MY BOOK OF
The
Elements

Adrian Dingle

DK | Penguin Random House

Editors John Hort, Niharika Prabhakar
Project editor Radhika Haswani
US editor Jill Hamilton
Senior US editor Shannon Beatty
Senior art editor Ann Cannings
Project art editor Bhagyashree Nayak
Assistant art editor Mansi Dwivedi
Illustrator Bettina Myklebust Stovne
Jacket designer Ann Cannings
DTP designers Dheeraj Singh,
Mohd Farhan
Senior picture researcher Sakshi Saluja
Production editor Becky Fallowfield
Senior production controller Ena Matagic
Managing editors Jonathan Melmoth,
Monica Saigal
Managing art editors Diane Peyton Jones,
Ivy Sengupta
Delhi creative head Malavika Talukder
Deputy art director Mabel Chan
Publishing director Sarah Larter

First American Edition, 2024
Published in the United States by DK Publishing
1745 Broadway, 20th Floor, New York, NY 10019

A catalog record for this book
is available from the Library of Congress.
ISBN 978-0-7440-9188-5

DK books are available at special discounts when
purchased in bulk for sales promotions, premiums,
fund-raising, or educational use. For details, contact:
DK Publishing Special Markets, 1745 Broadway,
20th Floor, New York, NY 10019
SpecialSales@dk.com

Printed and bound in China

www.dk.com

MIX
Paper | Supporting
responsible forestry
FSC™ C018179

This book was made with Forest
Stewardship Council™ certified
paper—one small step in DK's
commitment to a sustainable future.
For more information go to
www.dk.com/our-green-pledge

Contents

What is an element?

An element is a substance in its purest form. This means it cannot be broken down into more basic ingredients in a chemical reaction. Each element is made up of unique atoms, which are the building blocks of everything around us.

This diamond is a solid form of the element carbon. It contains only carbon atoms.

Most objects don't contain only one element. Rocks, for example, can contain many different ones.

In diamond, the carbon atoms are arranged in a crystal structure, which gives diamond a glassy appearance.

Building everything

Everything in the universe is made up of elements. There are 118 in total, including hydrogen, aluminum, and oxygen. Many elements can join with others to make compounds. Water is a compound—it is a combination of hydrogen and oxygen.

Ancient elements

Ancient Greek thinkers believed that the world had four elements: air, earth, fire, and water. It was only around 500 years ago that scientists learned that none of these were elements.

Human elements

The human body is almost entirely made from just six elements: oxygen, carbon, hydrogen, nitrogen, calcium, and phosphorus. But a total of 25 elements, called the "essential elements," are required to make our bodies work properly.

Oxygen makes up around 60 percent of mass in the body.

In solids, the particles are arranged in a very organized way. - - - -

In liquids, the particles can flow around one another freely.

In gases, the particles expand to fill the whole container, if there is one.

Forms

Matter can exist in three forms: as a solid, a liquid, or a gas. As the temperature of the particles increases from solid to liquid to gas, the particles have more energy and move around more.

Lightning can form a special state of matter in the atmosphere called *plasma*. Plasma is a charged gas.

Changing states

Most elements are solids at room temperature, but they can change from one state to another when they are heated or cooled. Changing the state does not change the element, just the energy of its particles.

Melting sulfur from a solid (top left) to a liquid (bottom right)

Atoms

Atoms are the smallest parts of any element that still have the same properties as the element. Atoms are made by combining three types of subatomic particle: positive protons, neutral neutrons, and negative electrons.

An average human hair is about 1 million atoms wide.

Six electrons move around the outside of the nucleus of this carbon atom.

This carbon atom has six neutrons in the nucleus (dense center) of the atom.

Six protons are also found in the nucleus.

Atomic structure

Sulfur atoms have 16 electrons. They are arranged in "shells" around the nucleus. Two in the first shell, eight in the next, and finally six in the outer shell. The outer electrons determine the chemical reactions of atoms.

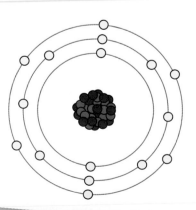

An element (such as helium, above) is defined by the number of protons it has, but the number of neutrons can vary. Atoms of a single element with differing numbers of neutrons are called isotopes.

The periodic table

The iconic periodic table is one of the most important tools that chemists have. It organizes the 118 elements by their atomic numbers into an ordered structure that can tell us a lot about each element.

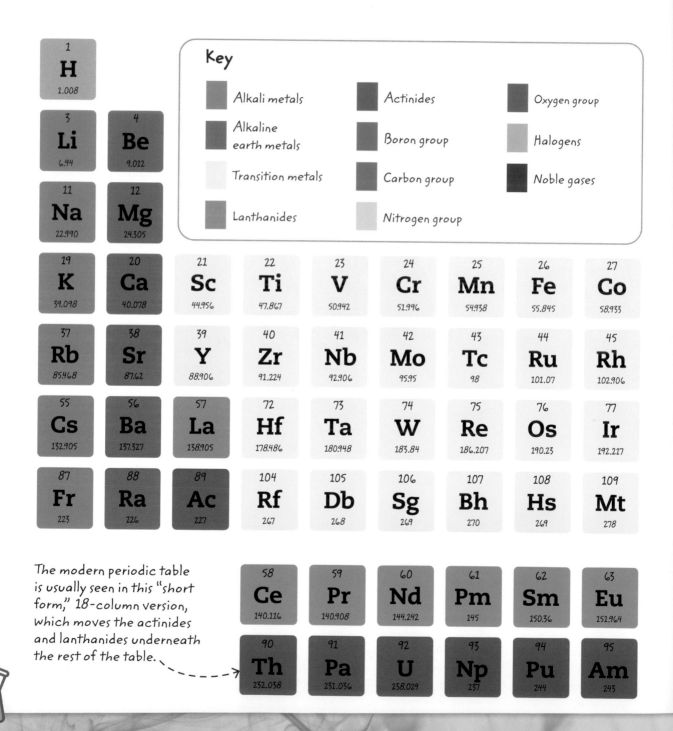

Key

- Alkali metals
- Alkaline earth metals
- Transition metals
- Lanthanides
- Actinides
- Boron group
- Carbon group
- Nitrogen group
- Oxygen group
- Halogens
- Noble gases

1 H 1.008									
3 Li 6.94	4 Be 9.012								
11 Na 22.990	12 Mg 24.305								
19 K 39.098	20 Ca 40.078	21 Sc 44.956	22 Ti 47.867	23 V 50.942	24 Cr 51.996	25 Mn 54.938	26 Fe 55.845	27 Co 58.933
37 Rb 85.468	38 Sr 87.62	39 Y 88.906	40 Zr 91.224	41 Nb 92.906	42 Mo 95.95	43 Tc 98	44 Ru 101.07	45 Rh 102.906
55 Cs 132.905	56 Ba 137.327	57 La 138.905	72 Hf 178.486	73 Ta 180.948	74 W 183.84	75 Re 186.207	76 Os 190.23	77 Ir 192.217
87 Fr 223	88 Ra 226	89 Ac 227	104 Rf 267	105 Db 268	106 Sg 269	107 Bh 270	108 Hs 269	109 Mt 278

The modern periodic table is usually seen in this "short form," 18-column version, which moves the actinides and lanthanides underneath the rest of the table.

| 58 Ce 140.116 | 59 Pr 140.908 | 60 Nd 144.242 | 61 Pm 145 | 62 Sm 150.36 | 63 Eu 151.964 |
| 90 Th 232.038 | 91 Pa 231.036 | 92 U 238.029 | 93 Np 237 | 94 Pu 244 | 95 Am 243 |

The top number is called the atomic number. It tells us the number of protons in one atom of the element.

Each element has a one- or two-letter symbol. If two letters are used, then the second is always lowercase.

2
He
4.003

The bottom number is not always shown, but is known as the atomic mass of the element.

The modern periodic table was proposed by chemist Dmitri Mendeleev.

2
He
4.003

Vertical columns on the table are called groups, and horizontal rows are called periods.

5	6	7	8	9	10
B	**C**	**N**	**O**	**F**	**Ne**
10.81	12.011	14.007	15.999	18.998	20.18

13	14	15	16	17	18
Al	**Si**	**P**	**S**	**Cl**	**Ar**
26.982	28.085	30.974	32.06	35.45	39.95

28	29	30	31	32	33	34	35	36
Ni	**Cu**	**Zn**	**Ga**	**Ge**	**As**	**Se**	**Br**	**Kr**
58.693	63.546	65.38	69.723	72.630	74.922	78.971	79.904	83.798

46	47	48	49	50	51	52	53	54
Pd	**Ag**	**Cd**	**In**	**Sn**	**Sb**	**Te**	**I**	**Xe**
106.42	107.868	112.414	114.818	118.710	121.76	127.6	126.904	131.293

78	79	80	81	82	83	84	85	86
Pt	**Au**	**Hg**	**Tl**	**Pb**	**Bi**	**Po**	**At**	**Rn**
195.084	196.967	200.592	204.38	207.2	208.98	209	210	222

110	111	112	113	114	115	116	117	118
Ds	**Rg**	**Cn**	**Nh**	**Fl**	**Mc**	**Lv**	**Ts**	**Og**
281	280	285	286	289	289	293	294	294

64	65	66	67	68	69	70	71
Gd	**Tb**	**Dy**	**Ho**	**Er**	**Tm**	**Yb**	**Lu**
157.25	158.925	162.5	164.93	167.259	168.934	173.045	174.967

96	97	98	99	100	101	102	103
Cm	**Bk**	**Cf**	**Es**	**Fm**	**Md**	**No**	**Lr**
247	247	251	252	257	258	259	262

The "long form" (with 32 columns) would be too wide to fit on this page.

Hydrogen

Hydrogen is the first element on the periodic table. It is the simplest and the lightest of all of the elements in the universe, and is the most plentiful, making up about 88 percent of all atoms.

The sun is approximately 75 percent hydrogen.

H — Fact file

» **Atomic number:** 1
» **Category:** Group 1
» **Melting point:** $-434\,°F$ $(-259\,°C)$
» **Discovery:** 1766
» **State at room temperature:** Gas

The sun releases heat and light energy when hydrogen atoms undergo a process called fusion.

Invisible gas

Pure hydrogen is a colorless, odorless, and tasteless gas. There isn't much elemental hydrogen on Earth, but lots of hydrogen atoms are found in compounds. Two out of every three atoms in a water molecule (H_2O) are hydrogen atoms.

Here, hydrogen gas is trapped in a glass sphere. The gas turns a purple color when electricity is passed through it.

In fusion, hydrogen atoms join together to make another element—helium.

Water is made up of two atoms of hydrogen (H) and one atom of oxygen (O) bonded together. Electricity can be used to release hydrogen gas (H_2) from water.

H																	He
Li	Be											B	C	N	O	F	Ne
Na	Mg											Al	Si	P	S	Cl	Ar
K	Ca	Sc	Ti	V	Cr	Mn	Fe	Co	Ni	Cu	Zn	Ga	Ge	As	Se	Br	Kr
Rb	Sr	Y	Zr	Nb	Mo	Tc	Ru	Rh	Pd	Ag	Cd	In	Sn	Sb	Te	I	Xe
Cs	Ba	La	Hf	Ta	W	Re	Os	Ir	Pt	Au	Hg	Tl	Pb	Bi	Po	At	Rn
Fr	Ra	Ac	Rf	Db	Sg	Bh	Hs	Mt	Ds	Rg	Cn	Nh	Fl	Mc	Lv	Ts	Og

Ce	Pr	Nd	Pm	Sm	Eu	Gd	Tb	Dy	Ho	Er	Tm	Yb	Lu
Th	Pa	U	Np	Pu	Am	Cm	Bk	Cf	Es	Fm	Md	No	Lr

The alkali metals are found in group 1, on the far left of the periodic table.

Metals lower in the group are more reactive than those near the top.

Alkali metals

The alkali metals are six shiny, soft metals with low melting points that are found naturally only in compounds. Their collective name comes from the fact that when they dissolve in water, a basic (alkaline) solution is produced.

Potassium ions give a distinct lilac color to a flame. Other ions give orange (sodium), various reds (lithium, rubidium), and blue (cesium).

Reactive

All the alkali metals are highly reactive elements. They will tarnish quickly in air by reacting with oxygen, and they react explosively with water. For this reason, they are usually stored in oil.

Lithium

Lithium is the lightest metal. Water is denser than lithium, so the metal will float on its surface. Lithium is extremely soft and can be cut with a knife easily.

- » **Atomic number:** 3
- » **Category:** Alkali metal
- » **Melting point:** 357 °F (181 °C)
- » **Discovery:** 1817
- » **State at room temperature:** Solid

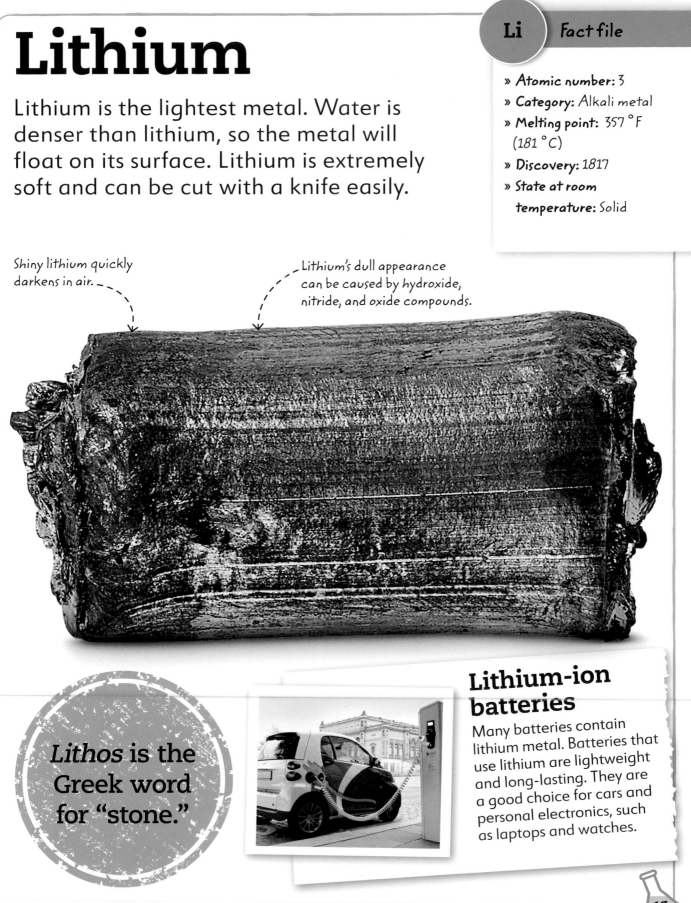

Shiny lithium quickly darkens in air.

Lithium's dull appearance can be caused by hydroxide, nitride, and oxide compounds.

Lithos is the Greek word for "stone."

Lithium-ion batteries

Many batteries contain lithium metal. Batteries that use lithium are lightweight and long-lasting. They are a good choice for cars and personal electronics, such as laptops and watches.

Sodium

Sodium is an important element in our bodies. It helps maintain a healthy blood pressure, and keeps our nerves and cells working properly. As a gas, it glows yellow in streetlamps when electricity is passed through it.

» **Atomic number:** 11
» **Category:** Alkali metal
» **Melting point:** 208 °F (98 °C)
» **Discovery:** 1807
» **State at room temperature:** Solid

This is sodium in its pure form. It is never found like this in nature, because it is so reactive.

Sodium reacts with the oxygen in the air and with water.

The salt that we put on food contains sodium. It is combined with the element chlorine in a compound called sodium chloride.

It is a soft metal that is easily cut with a butter knife.

Egyptian mummies

Sodium compounds were used during mummification, the process of preserving a dead body in ancient Egypt. Natron, a mixture of several sodium compounds, was stuffed into the body to dry it out and prevent further decay.

Potassium

Potassium is a dangerously reactive element. It is another soft metal that is usually stored in oil. The oil prevents it from coming into contact and reacting with air or water.

» **Atomic number:** 19
» **Category:** Alkali metal
» **Melting point:** 146 °F (64 °C)
» **Discovery:** 1807
» **State at room temperature:** Solid

When cut with a knife potassium is shiny, but it soon turns black when it reacts with oxygen in the air.

Potassium is too reactive to be found as a free element in nature.

Essential element

Potassium is a vital element for the human body. It helps muscles and nerves work properly. We need a few grams every day. Eating bananas is a great way to get the potassium you need.

When potassium reacts with oxygen, it forms potassium oxide.

Match heads contain potassium chlorate, a compound made up of potassium, chlorine, and oxygen ($KClO_3$).

Rubidium

Like its alkali metal family members, rubidium is a soft, reactive metal. It has a very low melting point, and could easily melt if placed in strong, summer sunlight.

Rubidium is a silvery-white metal.

Rubidium is held in a glass container to avoid a reaction with air. In air, it could burst into flames.

One particular type of rubidium isotope (Rb-82) is used in medical scans of human brains and hearts.

Night vision

Rubidium is sensitive to light. It is used in many special types of glass. These night-vision goggles contain rubidium as part of the lenses.

Rubidium will react with water, so the glass container also keeps it dry.

Cesium is a soft, shiny, gold-colored element.

It is solid at room temperature, but it would melt on a warm day.

Cesium

Cesium is one of the most reactive elements known and will react violently with water and the oxygen in the air. It is quite rare. The main source of cesium is an ore called pollucite.

Cs Fact file

» **Atomic number:** 55
» **Category:** Alkali metal
» **Melting point:** 83 °F (29 °C)
» **Discovery:** 1860
» **State at room temperature:** Solid

Francium

Francium is one of the rarest elements. Because it is so rare, it was one of the last elements to be discovered in nature. Francium has no uses other than in scientific research.

Francium can be extracted from an ore called uraninite.

Francium is formed in uraninite when other elements, such as actinium, break down.

Fr Fact file

» **Atomic number:** 87
» **Category:** Alkali metal
» **Melting point:** 70 °F (21 °C)
» **Discovery:** 1939
» **State at room temperature:** Solid

H																	He
Li	Be											B	C	N	O	F	Ne
Na	Mg											Al	Si	P	S	Cl	Ar
K	Ca	Sc	Ti	V	Cr	Mn	Fe	Co	Ni	Cu	Zn	Ga	Ge	As	Se	Br	Kr
Rb	Sr	Y	Zr	Nb	Mo	Tc	Ru	Rh	Pd	Ag	Cd	In	Sn	Sb	Te	I	Xe
Cs	Ba	La	Hf	Ta	W	Re	Os	Ir	Pt	Au	Hg	Tl	Pb	Bi	Po	At	Rn
Fr	Ra	Ac	Rf	Db	Sg	Bh	Hs	Mt	Ds	Rg	Cn	Nh	Fl	Mc	Lv	Ts	Og

Ce	Pr	Nd	Pm	Sm	Eu	Gd	Tb	Dy	Ho	Er	Tm	Yb	Lu
Th	Pa	U	Np	Pu	Am	Cm	Bk	Cf	Es	Fm	Md	No	Lr

The alkaline earth metals are found to the right-hand side of the alkali metals, in group 2 of the periodic table.

Each of the six elements is less reactive than its group 1 neighbor.

Alkaline earth metals

In early chemistry, certain substances were called "earths." At the time, earths were thought to be elements. Later, chemists found that earths were actually oxides of elements, like calcium, but the name stuck.

Ca(OH)2
Calcium Hydroxide Baked Lime

"Alkaline" means that they and their oxides dissolve in water to form bases (or alkalis), the chemical opposites of acids. One example is calcium hydroxide.

Health and hazards

The elements at the top and bottom of the group can be hazardous. Beryllium is toxic and radium is radioactive. The other elements are important for health, such as calcium and magnesium, which are vital for teeth among other things.

18

Beryllium

Beryllium can be a health hazard! Being exposed to beryllium for long periods can cause a lung disease called berylliosis. The subatomic particle, the neutron, was discovered by James Chadwick in 1932 by using beryllium.

The minerals beryl and bertrandite, which each contain silicon and oxygen, are good sources of beryllium metal.

High-tech metal

NASA's James Webb Space Telescope has mirrors that are made of beryllium, because it can withstand the cold temperatures of space. Beryllium is also used to make glass in helicopters, due to its lightness.

Beryllium is a soft, silvery-white metal.

It is a very light metal, with only lithium being lighter.

Magnesium

Magnesium is a light but strong metal. It is quite reactive, and extremely flammable and explosive when in powdered form. Magnesium fires can be spectacular and very dangerous.

Mg Fact file

- » **Atomic number:** 12
- » **Category:** Alkaline earth metal
- » **Melting point:** 1,202 °F (650 °C)
- » **Discovery:** 1755
- » **State at room temperature:** Solid

Magnesium exists as silver-colored crystals.

Magnesium burns in oxygen (air) with a brilliant white light.

Calcium confusion

Scottish chemist Joseph Black discovered magnesium. He also observed the difference between magnesium and calcium oxides — compounds that were until then thought to be the same.

Magnesium becomes dull when it reacts with oxygen in the air.

Calcium

Calcium is a very important metal for our health and the planet. It is the most abundant metal in the body and the fifth-most abundant element in Earth's crust.

Ca   *Fact file*

» **Atomic number:** 20
» **Category:** Alkaline earth metal
» **Melting point:** 1,548 °F (842 °C)
» **Discovery:** 1808
» **State at room temperature:** Solid

Aragonite

The metal is soft and can be cut with a knife.

Crystals of calcium metal can be grown in a laboratory.

Many minerals

Calcium is found mostly in compounds such as calcium oxide (CaO) and calcium hydroxide (Ca(OH)$_2$). Coral reefs contain lots of aragonite, which is made from calcium carbonate (CaCO$_3$).

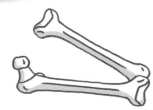

In the form of the compound calcium phosphate (Ca$_3$(PO$_4$)$_2$), the element gives human bones great strength.

Strontium

Strontium is a soft, silvery metal. It reacts with water to produce hydrogen gas. This element will burn in air and must be stored in glass or oil to protect it from reacting with oxygen.

| Sr | Fact file |

» **Atomic number:** 38
» **Category:** Alkaline earth metal
» **Melting point:** 777 °C (1,431 °F)
» **Discovery:** 1790
» **State at room temperature:** Solid

This strontium crystal was refined in a laboratory.

Barium

Barium's name comes from the Greek word *barys*, which means "heavy." In reality, barium is not that heavy an element, but some of its minerals are very dense. It is a reactive metal.

This barium crystal was made in a laboratory. Barium is so reactive that it is never found as a free metal in nature.

| Ba | Fact file |

» **Atomic number:** 56
» **Category:** Alkaline earth metal
» **Melting point:** 727 °C (1,341 °F)
» **Discovery:** 1808
» **State at room temperature:** Solid

Radium

Rare and radioactive, radium has a bad reputation as a dangerous element that causes cancer. It is a soft, shiny, and silver-colored metal that has no modern uses outside of research.

Radium comes from ores of uranium, such as uraninite.

This piece of uraninite contains very, very small amounts of radium.

Radium was once used to make watch faces that glowed in the dark.

Atoms of radium in uraninite break down quickly to create radon gas.

Discovery of radium

Radium was discovered by Marie and Pierre Curie in 1898. Much of Marie's work was with radioactive elements—she also discovered polonium. She won the Nobel Prize for Chemistry in 1911.

H																	He
Li	Be											B	C	N	O	F	Ne
Na	Mg											Al	Si	P	S	Cl	Ar
K	Ca	Sc	Ti	V	Cr	Mn	Fe	Co	Ni	Cu	Zn	Ga	Ge	As	Se	Br	Kr
Rb	Sr	Y	Zr	Nb	Mo	Tc	Ru	Rh	Pd	Ag	Cd	In	Sn	Sb	Te	I	Xe
Cs	Ba	La	Hf	Ta	W	Re	Os	Ir	Pt	Au	Hg	Tl	Pb	Bi	Po	At	Rn
Fr	Ra	Ac	Rf	Db	Sg	Bh	Hs	Mt	Ds	Rg	Cn	Nh	Fl	Mc	Lv	Ts	Og

		Ce	Pr	Nd	Pm	Sm	Eu	Gd	Tb	Dy	Ho	Er	Tm	Yb	Lu
		Th	Pa	U	Np	Pu	Am	Cm	Bk	Cf	Es	Fm	Md	No	Lr

This section of the periodic table is occasionally called the d-block.

Elements in group 12 (including Zn and Cd) are sometimes not thought of as transition metals.

Transition metals

Transition metals are found in the middle of the periodic table in groups 3 to 12, and periods 4 to 7. They are mostly hard metals with high melting points, and are good conductors of electricity.

Specialized uses

Many transition elements have special, high-tech uses. They are often used as catalysts that make reactions go faster, and in mixtures of metals called alloys.

Nitinol is an alloy of nickel and titanium and is known as a memory metal. Bend it, and it instantly returns to its original shape!

Scandium

Scandium is an important metal that is used in many alloys. It is often added to increase strength. With aluminum, it forms parts of fighter jets and guns.

—This pure scandium was made in a laboratory.

Alloys of scandium are used to make high-performance sports equipment, such as baseball bats and racing bikes.

Scandium is a soft, silvery metal. It tarnishes so it loses its shine quickly in air. — —

Fighter planes

Scandium is alloyed with aluminum to make military aircraft stronger and lighter. Lighter bodies mean that the planes are more fuel efficient.

25

Titanium

Titanium is named after the Titans, Greek gods known for their incredible strength. It is a fitting name, because titanium is one of the strongest transition metals. It is also quite light.

–This bar of titanium is made up of tiny silver crystals.

Titanium is used for metal screws and plates that support broken bones in the body.

Vanadium

Pure vanadium is soft and can be shaped and pulled into thin wires easily.

Vanadium is famous for making many colorful compounds. As a metal, it is added to steel to strengthen and harden it. It is also used in catalysts—compounds that speed up chemical reactions.

Chromium

Chromium is the shiny metal that is added to steel to make it "stainless." It was used on the outside of cars and motorcycles. Like other transition metals, it forms many colored compounds.

Its name comes from the Greek word chroma, meaning "color."

Chromium will stay shiny even when exposed to air and water.

Cr   Fact file

» **Atomic number:** 24
» **Category:** Transition metal
» **Melting point:** 3,465 °F (1,907 °C)
» **Discovery:** 1798
» **State at room temperature:** Solid

Rhodochrosite, a rose-colored rock, is one of the most common minerals of manganese.

Manganese

Manganese is found in many minerals. It is used in batteries and railroad tracks. A manganese compound is added to gasoline in place of lead because it is less toxic.

Mn   Fact file

» **Atomic number:** 25
» **Category:** Transition metal
» **Melting point:** 2,275 °F (1,246 °C)
» **Discovery:** 1774
» **State at room temperature:** Solid

Iron

In terms of its importance to civilization, iron has few competitors among other elements. Early tools and implements were made from it in the Iron Age, and modern buildings still rely on steel, an alloy that contains iron and carbon, for strength.

Fe Fact file

» **Atomic number:** 26
» **Category:** Transition metal
» **Melting point:** 2,800 °F (1,538 °C)
» **Discovery:** c. 3500 BCE
» **State at room temperature:** Solid

Smelting

Iron is extracted from its ores in a process called smelting. The carbon in coal is used to produce the pure, molten metal, which can then be poured into molds.

Cars are built using several alloys, including regular carbon steels and other special steels that include other elements.

This piece of pure iron was refined in a laboratory.

OVER 80 PERCENT OF THE EARTH'S CORE IS MADE UP OF IRON.

In its pure form, iron is brittle, meaning it does not flex or bend.

28

Cobalt

For hundreds of years, miners in Europe tried to extract silver from cobalt ores, but only succeeded in producing dangerous arsenic fumes. Because of this, cobalt is named after a German word for evil spirits, *kobald*.

» **Atomic number:** 27
» **Category:** Transition metal
» **Melting point:** 2,723 °F (1,495 °C)
» **Discovery:** 1739
» **State at room temperature:** Solid

Cobalt is silver-white in color.

It is a hard and shiny metal, but quite brittle.

One particular type of cobalt atom, the isotope cobalt-60, is used to irradiate food. This means it is used to preserve food by killing bacteria.

It is hard to tell cobalt from iron and nickel by appearance alone.

Cobalt blue

Cobalt has been used for centuries in coloring glass, and in the glazes for ceramic items, such as porcelain vases. It gives a very distinct color known as cobalt blue.

As well as blue, some cobalt compounds are pale pink.

29

Ni | Fact file

- » **Atomic number:** 28
- » **Category:** Transition metal
- » **Melting point:** 2,651 °F (1,455 °C)
- » **Discovery:** 1751
- » **State at room temperature:** Solid

The Hoba meteorite in Namibia is the largest found on Earth. It is made of iron and nickel.

Nickel

Nickel's name comes from the German word *kupfernickel*, meaning "copper demon." It was originally found in copper mines, in a reddish-brown ore that failed to produce copper. When nickel was eventually discovered in the ore, the name stuck.

Silver nickel

Nickel is used in alloys. It appears in stainless steel and is sometimes used to give a silver color to alloys or to achieve remarkable properties. For example, invar (iron and nickel) does not expand when heated.

These ball bearings are made from pure nickel. They are silver in color with a yellow tinge.

The center of Earth is also mainly iron and nickel, but mostly in a molten (melted) state.

The US five cent coin is a copper–nickel alloy and is known as a "nickel."

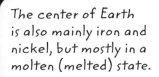

Copper

Copper is an instantly recognizable element, with its distinct red–brown color setting it apart from other metals. It is a great conductor of electricity, and a popular metal for making coins.

Here you can see branchlike crystals of copper metal growing on this mineral.

Cu | Fact file

» **Atomic number:** 29
» **Category:** Transition metal
» **Melting point:** 1,085 °C (1,984 °F)
» **Discovery:** 9000 BCE
» **State at room temperature:** Solid

Zinc

Zinc has many uses both on its own and in compounds. It is used to protect iron from corrosion in galvanized steel, and as zinc oxide it is used as sunscreen.

A typical silver–gray metal, zinc is often found in nature with lead and silver.

This metal is quite reactive, corroding in air very easily.

Zn | Fact file

» **Atomic number:** 30
» **Category:** Transition metal
» **Melting point:** 420 °C (787 °F)
» **Discovery:** 1746
» **State at room temperature:** Solid

Yttrium

Y | Fact file

» **Atomic number:** 39
» **Category:** Transition metal
» **Melting point:** 1,522 °C (2,772 °F)
» **Discovery:** 1794
» **State at room temperature:** Solid

Yttrium is one of the four elements named after the Swedish town of Ytterby. Yttrium has some weird and wonderful compounds, including YAG (yttrium-aluminum-garnet), which is used in medical lasers.

Yttrium is a soft, silvery-white metal.

Zirconium

Zr | Fact file

» **Atomic number:** 40
» **Category:** Transition metal
» **Melting point:** 1,854 °C (3,369 °F)
» **Discovery:** 1789
» **State at room temperature:** Solid

Zirconium is a very hard metal. This makes it useful as part of many alloys. Zirconium dioxide is used to make ceramic dental crowns, and cubic zirconia can be used as a substitute for diamonds.

Pure zirconium is shiny.

Niobium

Nb | Fact file

» **Atomic number:** 41
» **Category:** Transition metal
» **Melting point:** 2,477 °C (4,491 °F)
» **Discovery:** 1801
» **State at room temperature:** Solid

Niobium is a metal that is used in many alloys. It is also used in magnets for MRI machines. Before 1950, it was known as columbium (Cb).

This element is shiny and gray.

Molybdenum

Molybdenum is a tough metal. It is added to steel to make it stronger and harder. These alloys are called "moly steels." This element is used in catalysts in the oil industry.

Molybdenum is extracted from molybdenite, a soft mineral.

Molybdenite is similar to graphite, and both have been used as the "lead" in pencils and as lubricants.

Technetium

Technetium's name comes from the Greek word *tekhnetos*, meaning "artificial," as it was the first artificially produced element. It was discovered by Carlo Perrier and Emilio Segrè. The element is used in medical tests.

Technetium is a silver-colored metal, but it can also be obtained as a gray powder.

This sample of pure technetium was made in a nuclear reactor.

Ruthenium

Ruthenium is a relatively rare metal that finds use as a catalyst. One of its compounds, ruthenium dioxide, is found in electronics. It is mixed with softer metals, such as platinum, to make them harder.

It is a shiny, silvery-white metal.

Rhodium is so shiny that it is used in headlight reflectors and optical mirrors.

Rhodium

Rhodium is a very rare element, which makes it one of the most expensive metals in the world. Like ruthenium, it is also used as a catalyst. Rhodium is often used in jewelry.

Palladium

Palladium is an important catalyst. It has an unusual ability to absorb hydrogen gas, which means that it could be used to transport the gas without the need for high pressure.

It is a shiny, gray metal that can be shaped and drawn into wires easily.

Silver

Silver has an ancient history as a precious metal. Used for centuries as currency, and as a decorative metal in jewelry and other items like cutlery, its shiny nature has always been attractive to humans.

A common compound of silver has been used as a wart remover.

Use in gadgets

Like many other similar precious metals, silver is used in modern electronic devices, mainly because it is an excellent conductor of electricity.

Silver can be extracted from ores, but is also found in its pure metal state.

Silver is known for its shiny appearance, but it quickly turns black when exposed to air.

In South Asia, silver foil is used as a decorative, edible coating on sweets, and is called vark.

Cadmium

This soft metal's compounds have a history of being used as pigments in art. Unfortunately, it was discovered that cadmium is a nasty, poisonous element, so it has been banned from use in paints.

This is a soft pellet of pure cadmium.

Cd Fact file

» **Atomic number:** 48
» **Category:** Transition metal
» **Melting point:** 321 °C (610 °F)
» **Discovery:** 1817
» **State at room temperature:** Solid

Hf Fact file

» **Atomic number:** 72
» **Category:** Transition metal
» **Melting point:** 2,233 °C (4,051 °F)
» **Discovery:** 1923
» **State at room temperature:** Solid

Hafnium is a silvery, shiny metal.

Hafnium

Hafnium is a very hard metal. It was tricky to find, being the second most recent of the naturally occurring elements discovered. Its name comes from *Hafnia*, the Latin name for the city of Copenhagen, Denmark, where it was found.

Tantalum

Tantalum is named after King Tantalus in Greek mythology. It is a metal that is nontoxic and resistant to corrosion. These properties make it an ideal choice for artificial joints in the body.

It is a tough, shiny, silver-colored metal.

Ta Fact file

» **Atomic number:** 73
» **Category:** Transition metal
» **Melting point:** 3,017 °C (5,463 °F)
» **Discovery:** 1802
» **State at room temperature:** Solid

Tungsten

Tungsten is a hard, dense element with the highest melting point of all metals. These properties make it suitable for many uses, such as in the filaments of light bulbs or in rocket engines.

Pure tungsten is a grayish-white metal that is shiny.

Tungsten is brittle and loses its shine in air.

Rhenium is a silver-colored metal that is very dense.

It is usually produced in the form of a fine powder.

Rhenium

Rhenium is rare, and was one of the last naturally occurring elements to be discovered. Like its neighbors on the periodic table, it has a high melting point.

Osmium

Os Fact file

» **Atomic number:** 76
» **Category:** Transition metal
» **Melting point:** 3,033 °C (5,491 °F)
» **Discovery:** 1803
» **State at room temperature:** Solid

Osmium is the most dense of all the elements. Although osmium is a hard, tough element with a high melting point, it is brittle and can shatter easily.

Iridium

This is a pure pellet of iridium metal made in the laboratory.

Ir Fact file

» **Atomic number:** 77
» **Category:** Transition metal
» **Melting point:** 2,446 °C (4,435 °F)
» **Discovery:** 1803
» **State at room temperature:** Solid

Iridium is a very rare element on Earth. A hard, shiny, and brittle metal, it is incredibly dense, with only its periodic table neighbor, osmium, being more dense.

Platinum

Platinum is a silvery-white metal that is resistant to corrosion.

Pt Fact file

» **Atomic number:** 78
» **Category:** Transition metal
» **Melting point:** 1,768 °C (3,215 °F)
» **Discovery:** 1735
» **State at room temperature:** Solid

Platinum is an unreactive metal. It was discovered in the middle of the 18th century in South America, where it was known as *platina*, meaning "little silver" in Spanish.

39

Gold

With its distinct color and incredible shine, gold is perhaps the most recognizable of all the elements. The earliest chemists (the alchemists) spent much of their time trying to turn other metals into gold.

Au | Fact file

- » **Atomic number:** 79
- » **Category:** Transition metal
- » **Melting point:** 1,948 °F (1,064 °C)
- » **Discovery:** c. 3000 BCE
- » **State at room temperature:** Solid

Found in nature in its pure form, gold is quite a soft metal.

Jewelry

Gold has been used as jewelry as well as in decorations, ornaments, and sculptures for thousands of years. Because it is soft, it is easy to form into shapes. Metals that can be shaped easily are described as malleable.

This is the golden mask of the ancient Egyptian pharaoh Tutankhamun.

These are gold earrings from the Ptolemaic Period found in Tell Dafana, Egypt.

Electronics

Gold is used in many common electronic devices. It is often used as a connector because it is a good conductor of electricity and is resistant to corrosion.

Gold can be found inside laptop computers. When electronics are recycled, the metal is sometimes recovered.

Gold metal can be found in smartphones, too.

Large gold nuggets like this one are rare.

Money

Throughout history, gold has been used as money. From ancient to modern times, people have been able to exchange the precious metal for goods and services.

A Byzantine gold coin

California Gold Rush

The California Gold Rush of 1848–1855 brought approximately 300,000 people to the west coast of the US to seek gold. The prospectors were called "forty-niners," since most of the people arrived in 1849.

The Gold Rush prospectors

Mercury

Mercury has interested people for centuries, including the alchemists who tried to transform some metals into more valuable ones. However, mercury is a nasty poison.

Mercury is one of only two elements that are liquids at room temperature.

It is called quicksilver for its color and its ability to move and be poured.

Rutherfordium

Rutherfordium was named after the famous scientist Ernest Rutherford from New Zealand.

Rutherfordium is an artificial element that was first made in a laboratory. It is radioactive, and even its longest-living isotope lasts for only a few minutes.

Dubnium

Dubnium is named after the Russian city where it was first made, Dubna. All of its isotopes are radioactive, and the element has no known uses outside of research in specialized laboratories.

Jim Harris and Albert Ghiorso were part of an American team that discovered it in 1970.

Db Fact file

» **Atomic number:** 105
» **Category:** Transition metal
» **Melting point:** Unknown
» **Discovery:** 1968
» **State at room temperature:** Solid

Seaborgium

Sg Fact file

» **Atomic number:** 106
» **Category:** Transition metal
» **Melting point:** Unknown
» **Discovery:** 1974
» **State at room temperature:** Solid

Seaborgium has no uses outside of research. When it was first produced, by smashing together californium and oxygen nuclei, only a few atoms of it were made.

Seaborgium is named after the nuclear chemist Glenn T. Seaborg.

Bohrium

Bohrium was first produced in a particle accelerator, when chromium and bismuth atoms were crashed into one another at high speed. Element 107 wasn't officially named until 16 years later.

Bohrium is named after the famous Danish physicist Niels Bohr.

Bh Fact file

» **Atomic number:** 107
» **Category:** Transition metal
» **Melting point:** Unknown
» **Discovery:** 1981
» **State at room temperature:** Solid

The German scientist Peter Armbruster led the team that discovered hassium, along with his fellow physicist Gottfried Münzenberg.

Hassium

Hassium is an artificially produced, radioactive element that is named after the German state of Hesse, where it was first made at the GSI Helmholtz Centre for Heavy Ion Research.

Hs Fact file

- » **Atomic number:** 108
- » **Category:** Transition metal
- » **Melting point:** Unknown
- » **Discovery:** 1984
- » **State at room temperature:** Solid

Meitnerium

Element number 109 was named in honor of the Austrian physicist Lise Meitner.

This artificial, radioactive element has no uses outside of chemical research. It was first produced in Germany when bismuth and iron atoms were made to collide in a particle accelerator.

Mt Fact file

- » **Atomic number:** 109
- » **Category:** Transition metal
- » **Melting point:** Unknown
- » **Discovery:** 1982
- » **State at room temperature:** Solid

Darmstadtium

Darmstadtium is another artificial, radioactive element. It was first created by smashing nickel atoms into lead atoms. It is named after the German city of Darmstadt.

Sigurd Hofmann led the team that made this element in Germany.

Ds — Fact file

» **Atomic number:** 110
» **Category:** Transition metal
» **Melting point:** Unknown
» **Discovery:** 1994
» **State at room temperature:** Solid

Rg — Fact file

» **Atomic number:** 111
» **Category:** Transition metal
» **Melting point:** Unknown
» **Discovery:** 1994
» **State at room temperature:** Solid

Roentgenium

Roentgenium is in the same group as gold. Some chemists think that it may have similar properties to gold. Only a few atoms have ever been made.

Element number 111 is named after the German physicist Wilhelm Röntgen.

Copernicium

A few atoms of copernicium were first made at the GSI Helmholtz Centre for Heavy Ion Research in the city of Darmstadt, Germany. They were made by smashing zinc and lead atoms together.

Copernicium is named after the astronomer Nicolaus Copernicus.

Cn — Fact file

» **Atomic number:** 112
» **Category:** Transition metal
» **Melting point:** Unknown
» **Discovery:** 1996
» **State at room temperature:** Solid

H																	He
Li	Be											B	C	N	O	F	Ne
Na	Mg											Al	Si	P	S	Cl	Ar
K	Ca	Sc	Ti	V	Cr	Mn	Fe	Co	Ni	Cu	Zn	Ga	Ge	As	Se	Br	Kr
Rb	Sr	Y	Zr	Nb	Mo	Tc	Ru	Rh	Pd	Ag	Cd	In	Sn	Sb	Te	I	Xe
Cs	Ba	La	Hf	Ta	W	Re	Os	Ir	Pt	Au	Hg	Tl	Pb	Bi	Po	At	Rn
Fr	Ra	Ac	Rf	Db	Sg	Bh	Hs	Mt	Ds	Rg	Cn	Nh	Fl	Mc	Lv	Ts	Og

The lanthanides are found in the f-block of the periodic table.

Ce	Pr	Nd	Pm	Sm	Eu	Gd	Tb	Dy	Ho	Er	Tm	Yb	Lu
Th	Pa	U	Np	Pu	Am	Cm	Bk	Cf	Es	Fm	Md	No	Lr

The f-block also includes the actinides.

Lanthanides

The lanthanides are a set of 15 elements that have become very important in modern life. Sometimes they (along with a few other elements) are referred to as "rare earth elements," but that is misleading, because many of them are not that rare.

High-tech electronics

Many of the lanthanides are used in modern electronics, such as camera lenses, lasers, magnets, and medicine. As a result, they are often in high demand.

The lanthanides proved difficult to discover. They are all similar and were difficult to separate from one another. The mineral bastnäsite, for example, contains multiple lanthanides.

Lanthanum

Lanthanum is the element that the lanthanides are named after. Lanthanide means "like lanthanum." It is used to find the age of old rocks, and in the treatment of kidney disease.

This metal is soft and can be cut with a knife easily.

La — Fact file

» **Atomic number:** 57
» **Category:** Lanthanide
» **Melting point:** 920 °C (1,688 °F)
» **Discovery:** 1839
» **State at room temperature:** Solid

Cerium

Ce — Fact file

» **Atomic number:** 58
» **Category:** Lanthanide
» **Melting point:** 799 °C (1,470 °F)
» **Discovery:** 1803
» **State at room temperature:** Solid

Cerium is named after a dwarf planet, Ceres. Its oxide is used in catalytic converters in cars to change harmful fumes into less harmful ones.

Cerium is a gray-colored metal that can be scratched easily.

Praseodymium

Praseodymium started life as an "element" that was given the name didymium. It was later found that didymium was made up of two elements, praseodymium and neodymium.

Praseodymium is a soft, dark gray metal in its pure form.

Pr — Fact file

» **Atomic number:** 59
» **Category:** Lanthanide
» **Melting point:** 931 °C (1,708 °F)
» **Discovery:** 1885
» **State at room temperature:** Solid

Neodymium

Neodymium is best known for its use in extremely strong magnets. When combined with iron and boron, the strongest-known magnets are created. Neodymium is also used in medical lasers.

Neodymium is a silvery-white metal, but it rapidly reacts with oxygen in the air and turns black.

Promethium

Promethium is a radioactive element that has long since decayed away from natural sources. It has been used in special batteries and as a power source in missiles.

Radioactive promethium was once used in glow-in-the-dark paint.

Samarium

Samarium is named after the mineral from which it was first extracted, samarskite. It can be combined with cobalt metal in an alloy to make sensitive magnets used in speakers.

Samarium is a silvery-white metal.

Europium

The element europium was named after the continent of Europe. It was discovered in France. It is added to the special inks used to print banknotes. The ink glows under ultraviolet light, making banknotes difficult to copy.

Europium takes on many beautiful colors when exposed to air.

Eu Fact file

» **Atomic number:** 63
» **Category:** Lanthanide
» **Melting point:** 822 °C (1,512 °F)
» **Discovery:** 1901
» **State at room temperature:** Solid

Gd Fact file

» **Atomic number:** 64
» **Category:** Lanthanide
» **Melting point:** 1,313 °C (2,395 °F)
» **Discovery:** 1880
» **State at room temperature:** Solid

Gadolinium

This element was named after the famous Finnish chemist Johan Gadolin, who was an expert on the lanthanides. Gadolinium is used in MRI scans in medicine to improve picture quality.

It forms a dark, flaky oxide layer when exposed to air.

Terbium

Terbium was confused with the element erbium for a long time. It can be used to produce green colors in television screens, and is also used in low-energy light bulbs.

Terbium is a dark, very soft metal that can be cut by a knife easily.

Tb Fact file

» **Atomic number:** 65
» **Category:** Lanthanide
» **Melting point:** 1,359 °C (2,478 °F)
» **Discovery:** 1843
» **State at room temperature:** Solid

Dysprosium

Dysprosium metal's main use is in alloys with other lanthanide elements. These alloys are used to make powerful magnets. The superstrong magnets are used in wind turbines and electric motors.

A pure sample of dysprosium metal is shiny.

Holmium

Like several of the lanthanides, holmium is used to make specialized magnets. When found in nature, it often causes minerals to have a red or yellow color, and it can be used to color glass.

It is a shiny, soft metal.

Erbium

Erbium can be used in glass that absorbs infrared radiation. This glass is then used in safety goggles for welders, as it stops the infrared radiation from reaching and damaging the eyes.

Pure erbium is soft, and silvery-white in color.

Thulium

Thulium has a couple of useful applications in medicine. Small samples of it can be used in portable X-ray machines, and it is used in surgical lasers. It is one of the rarest of the lanthanides.

Pure thulium is silvery-gray in color.

Tm Fact file

» **Atomic number:** 69
» **Category:** Lanthanide
» **Melting point:** 1,545 °C (2,813 °F)
» **Discovery:** 1879
» **State at room temperature:** Solid

Ytterbium

Yb Fact file

» **Atomic number:** 70
» **Category:** Lanthanide
» **Melting point:** 824 °C (1,515 °F)
» **Discovery:** 1878
» **State at room temperature:** Solid

Ytterbium is one of four elements named after a small town in Sweden, Ytterby—the others are yttrium, terbium, and erbium. Ytterbium is used in modern catalysts of various types.

This is a lab sample of pure ytterbium.

Lutetium

Lutetium is one of the most expensive metals in the world. It is mainly used for research and has very few applications, but it is used in the oil and gas industry as a catalyst.

It is a hard, silvery, dense metal.

Lu Fact file

» **Atomic number:** 71
» **Category:** Lanthanide
» **Melting point:** 1,663 °C (3,025 °F)
» **Discovery:** 1907
» **State at room temperature:** Solid

H																	He
Li	Be											B	C	N	O	F	Ne
Na	Mg											Al	Si	P	S	Cl	Ar
K	Ca	Sc	Ti	V	Cr	Mn	Fe	Co	Ni	Cu	Zn	Ga	Ge	As	Se	Br	Kr
Rb	Sr	Y	Zr	Nb	Mo	Tc	Ru	Rh	Pd	Ag	Cd	In	Sn	Sb	Te	I	Xe
Cs	Ba	La	Hf	Ta	W	Re	Os	Ir	Pt	Au	Hg	Tl	Pb	Bi	Po	At	Rn
Fr	Ra	Ac	Rf	Db	Sg	Bh	Hs	Mt	Ds	Rg	Cn	Nh	Fl	Mc	Lv	Ts	Og

		Ce	Pr	Nd	Pm	Sm	Eu	Gd	Tb	Dy	Ho	Er	Tm	Yb	Lu
		Th	Pa	U	Np	Pu	Am	Cm	Bk	Cf	Es	Fm	Md	No	Lr

The actinides are found at the very bottom of the periodic table.

They are part of the section of the periodic table known as the f-block.

Actinides

The actinides are a collection of highly radioactive elements. Many of them are only created artificially, and those that occur in nature are often quite rare and are the result of other elements decaying.

Six of the actinides are named after people, three after places, and three after planets (or dwarf planets). Neptunium, for example, is named after Neptune.

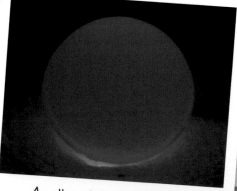

A pellet of plutonium oxide

Transuranium elements

There was a time when the periodic table was thought to end at element 92, uranium. Since then, another 26 elements have been either found in nature or artificially made. These are called the transuranium elements. Plutonium is a transuranium element.

Actinium

There are only tiny amounts of actinium present in Earth's crust. That's because all of actinium's isotopes are very radioactive and decay away quickly. Most are made artificially by colliding radium atoms with neutrons.

Ac Fact file

» **Atomic number:** 89
» **Category:** Actinide
» **Melting point:** 1,922 °F (1,050 °C)
» **Discovery:** 1899
» **State at room temperature:** Solid

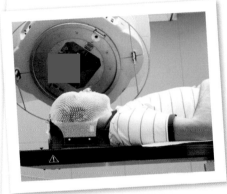

Radiotherapy
Actinium is a radioactive element and as such does not have many applications, but the radioactivity of one of its isotopes is used in some cancer treatments.

Greek *actinos*, meaning "ray," gives actinium its name.

Uraninite contains uranium, which breaks down naturally to produce very tiny amounts of actinium.

Several tons of uraninite contain only a few milligrams of actinium.

Actinium can be found in the bright yellow mineral autunite, which glows in ultraviolet light.

Thorium

Thorium is a dangerous element. Oddly, at the beginning of the 20th century, it was sold as a medicine that claimed to cure all kinds of disease. Unfortunately, it only succeeded in causing many health issues.

Monazite is the chief ore of thorium and comes in many colors from yellow to red–brown.

Th Fact file

- » **Atomic number:** 90
- » **Category:** Actinide
- » **Melting point:** 1,750 °C (3,182 °F)
- » **Discovery:** 1829
- » **State at room temperature:** Solid

Protactinium

The mineral torbernite contains uranium, which naturally decays to produce protactinium.

Protactinium's name comes from *protos* (Greek for "first") and element number 89 (actinium), because it is formed before actinium when uranium decays. It has no known uses outside of research.

Pa Fact file

- » **Atomic number:** 91
- » **Category:** Actinide
- » **Melting point:** 1,572 °C (2,862 °F)
- » **Discovery:** 1913
- » **State at room temperature:** Solid

» **Atomic number:** 92
» **Category:** Actinide
» **Melting point:** 1,135 °C (2,075 °F)
» **Discovery:** 1789
» **State at room temperature:** Solid

Uranium is a metallic element and silver–gray in color.

Uranium

Uranium is the most common nuclear fuel. Splitting uranium atoms apart, in a process called fission, releases huge amounts of energy that can be used for power, or as a weapon in nuclear bombs.

Uraninite is a mineral that contains mostly uranium, but also some neptunium.

» **Atomic number:** 93
» **Category:** Actinide
» **Melting point:** 644 °C (1,191 °F)
» **Discovery:** 1940
» **State at room temperature:** Solid

Neptunium

Just like its neighbor on the periodic table, neptunium was also named after a planet. It was discovered by Edwin M. McMillian, who later won the Nobel Prize in Chemistry.

Plutonium

Plutonium is a radioactive element that has played a huge role in history. It formed part of the Little Boy and Fat Man nuclear bombs used in World War II. It is still used in nuclear reactors today.

This picture shows a radioactive pellet of plutonium oxide glowing.

The orange glow is a result of radioactive decay, which produces heat energy.

Using plutonium

In the last century, plutonium had a wide range of uses. The element was used in the exploration of the universe, in healthcare, and during wars.

Curiosity rover

Spacecraft power

The heat produced by the decay of plutonium can be converted to electricity. NASA uses plutonium in this way to power spacecraft such as *Voyager* and *Pioneer*, robot landers such as Mars Pathfinder, and rovers such as the Mars Curiosity Rover.

Fact file

» **Atomic number:** 94
» **Category:** Actinide
» **Melting point:** 1,184 °F (640 °C)
» **Discovery:** 1940
» **State at room temperature:** Solid

Plutonium has several isotopes, all of which are radioactive.

Early pacemakers
Some of the early heart pacemakers—devices put into humans to help their hearts beat correctly—had plutonium batteries.

Nuclear weapons
The *Fat Man* atomic bomb was dropped on the Japanese city of Nagasaki in 1945. It carried around 14 lb (6.2 kg) of plutonium.

Americium

Americium was first made in a laboratory at the University of Chicago, US. It is a radioactive element that only occurs naturally on Earth in trace (tiny) amounts.

Americium is used in smoke detectors, like the one below. Smoke interferes with the particles that are produced by the detector, sounding an alarm.

Am | Fact file

- » **Atomic number:** 95
- » **Category:** Actinide
- » **Melting point:** 1,176 °C (2,149 °F)
- » **Discovery:** 1944
- » **State at room temperature:** Solid

Curium

Curium was discovered in the US as part of research into nuclear weapons during World War II. Its discovery had to be kept secret until the end of the war for security reasons.

Curium wasn't discovered by Marie and Pierre Curie, but it was named in their honor for their pioneering work in radioactivity.

Cm | Fact file

- » **Atomic number:** 96
- » **Category:** Actinide
- » **Melting point:** 1,345 °C (2,453 °F)
- » **Discovery:** 1944
- » **State at room temperature:** Solid

Berkelium

Berkelium is a radioactive, silver-colored metal that has no known uses outside of research. A few atoms of the element were first made by bombarding the element americium with helium.

This element is named after the city of Berkeley, California, US.

Bk — Fact file

» **Atomic number:** 97
» **Category:** Actinide
» **Melting point:** 986 °C (1,807 °F)
» **Discovery:** 1949
» **State at room temperature:** Solid

Californium

Californium has been used in cancer treatment and in nuclear military applications. It has more than 20 different isotopes, all of which are radioactive.

These silver-colored pellets contain californium metal.

Californium is malleable, and is a relatively soft metal.

Cf — Fact file

» **Atomic number:** 98
» **Category:** Actinide
» **Melting point:** 900 °C (1,652 °F)
» **Discovery:** 1950
» **State at room temperature:** Solid

Einsteinium

Einsteinium was discovered in the remains of the first hydrogen bomb test, "Ivy Mike." In that huge explosion, other smaller atoms were forced together to make atoms of the new element.

» **Atomic number:** 99
» **Category:** Actinide
» **Melting point:** 860 °C (1,580 °F)
» **Discovery:** 1952
» **State at room temperature:** Solid

Einsteinium is named after the famous physicist Albert Einstein.

Einstein won the Nobel Prize in Physics in 1921.

Fermium

Element 100 is named after Enrico Fermi, an Italian physicist.

$$\alpha = \frac{\hbar^2}{ec}$$

Just like its neighbor on the periodic table, einsteinium, fermium was first discovered in the remains of the "Ivy Mike" hydrogen bomb test. Only a few atoms of fermium were made in the blast.

Fm Fact file

» **Atomic number:** 100
» **Category:** Actinide
» **Melting point:** 1,527 °C (2,781 °F)
» **Discovery:** 1953
» **State at room temperature:** Solid

Mendelevium

Mendelevium was first produced in California, US, by smashing atoms of einsteinium and helium together. The element is radioactive and has no known uses.

» **Atomic number:** 101
» **Category:** Actinide
» **Melting point:** 827 °C (1,521 °F)
» **Discovery:** 1955
» **State at room temperature:** Solid

Mendelevium is named after the father of the modern periodic table, Dmitri Mendeleev.

Nobelium

No   Fact file

» **Atomic number:** 102
» **Category:** Actinide
» **Melting point:** 827 °C (1,521 °F)
» **Discovery:** 1963
» **State at room temperature:** Solid

Nobelium is a radioactive element with no known uses outside of chemical research. Several groups claimed to have discovered the element for the first time, and even a different name—joliotium—was proposed.

Element 102 is named after Alfred Nobel, the founder of the Nobel Prize.

Lawrencium

Lawrencium was made one atom at a time by scientists in California, US. Boron with 5 protons, and californium with 98, were smashed into one another to create the new atom.

Lr   Fact file

» **Atomic number:** 103
» **Category:** Actinide
» **Melting point:** 1,627 °C (2,961 °F)
» **Discovery:** 1965
» **State at room temperature:** Solid

The element was named after American nuclear physicist Ernest O. Lawrence.

H																	He
Li	Be											B	C	N	O	F	Ne
Na	Mg											Al	Si	P	S	Cl	Ar
K	Ca	Sc	Ti	V	Cr	Mn	Fe	Co	Ni	Cu	Zn	Ga	Ge	As	Se	Br	Kr
Rb	Sr	Y	Zr	Nb	Mo	Tc	Ru	Rh	Pd	Ag	Cd	In	Sn	Sb	Te	I	Xe
Cs	Ba	La	Hf	Ta	W	Re	Os	Ir	Pt	Au	Hg	Tl	Pb	Bi	Po	At	Rn
Fr	Ra	Ac	Rf	Db	Sg	Bh	Hs	Mt	Ds	Rg	Cn	Nh	Fl	Mc	Lv	Ts	Og

Ce	Pr	Nd	Pm	Sm	Eu	Gd	Tb	Dy	Ho	Er	Tm	Yb	Lu
Th	Pa	U	Np	Pu	Am	Cm	Bk	Cf	Es	Fm	Md	No	Lr

Elements in the boron group are called the "post-transition metals" because they appear directly after those elements.

The boron group is known as group 13.

Boron group

Group 13 includes at least one very familiar element, aluminum, as well as several less well-known ones, such as nihonium. Boron is a metalloid. Little is known about nihonium, but the others (Al, Ga, In, and Tl) are all silvery-white, soft metals.

Soyuz spacecraft

High-tech metals

Aluminum, gallium, and indium are metals that are used in many high-tech and specialized applications. From aircraft and spacecraft to semiconductors, many aspects of the tech and electronics industries depend on these elements.

The group has been called the icosagens because atoms of the elements can form an unusual shape called an icosahedron.

Boron

Boron is a semimetal or metalloid. This means it sometimes acts like a metal and sometimes like a nonmetal. It is a tough element that is used to strengthen materials and make heat-resistant glass.

B   Fact file

» **Atomic number:** 5
» **Category:** Boron group
» **Melting point:** 3,771 °F (2,077 °C)
» **Discovery:** 1808
» **State at room temperature:** Solid

Boron is very unreactive, so it stays the same color in air.

Boron compounds have been used to make green fireworks.

Uses at home

Boron is a common element in the home. It appears in TV and laptop screens and In kitchen glassware. As borax (a compound of boron, sodium, and oxygen), it can be found in many laundry products.

Boron is dark gray in color with a slightly shiny appearance.

It is quite hard and has a very high melting point.

63

Aluminum

Aluminum is the most common metal element in Earth's crust. It is a strong and light metal that is used in construction. It is also an excellent conductor of electricity.

» **Atomic number:** 13
» **Category:** Boron group
» **Melting point:** 1,221 °F (660 °C)
» **Discovery:** 1825
» **State at room temperature:** Solid

These are chunks of pure aluminum metal.

Chunks of aluminum can be pressed into a thin foil for food packaging.

Smartwatches and smartphones often have aluminum cases that are lightweight but strong, so they protect the devices.

It is a shiny, reflective metal.

Transportation

Since aluminum is strong and lightweight, it is often used in making bicycles, spacecraft, cars, aircraft, and boats. It is also resistant to corrosion.

Gallium

Gallium is a high-tech metal that is similar to its neighbor in the periodic table, aluminum. It can be found in solar panels, LEDs, and in semiconductors in the electronics industry.

Ga   Fact file

» **Atomic number:** 31
» **Category:** Boron group
» **Melting point:** 86 °F (30 °C)
» **Discovery:** 1875
» **State at room temperature:** Solid

Gallium is a soft, silvery-white metal that is solid at room temperature.

If you hold this metal in your hand, your body heat will cause it to melt.

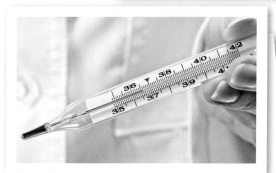

Galinstan

For many years, mercury metal was used in thermometers and barometers. However, mercury comes with lots of health hazards. A liquid alloy of gallium, called galinstan, can be used as an alternative.

Gallium is used to make alloys with low melting points.

The name comes from *Gallia*, the Latin name for France, where it was discovered.

Indium

Indium is named after a color, indigo. When electricity is passed through indium gas, an indigo color is seen. The metal appears in low-melting point alloys, such as those used in fire-sprinkler systems.

Several compounds of indium produce a bright, blue–purple color when heated in an open flame.

Touchscreens
The most common use of indium metal in the modern world is in touchscreens. Phones and computers use a material called indium tin oxide, or ITO.

Like its neighbor, gallium, indium is a soft, shiny, silver-colored metal.

When indium metal is bent, it makes a shrieking noise.

It can be cut with a knife easily.

Thallium

Thallium has a reputation as a very dangerous element. It is extremely toxic to humans. Thallium's name comes from the Greek word *thallos*, meaning "green shoot," as it emits a green color in its spectrum.

This sample of pure thallium is kept in a sealed tube because it is highly toxic.

Thallium is a soft but heavy, silvery metal that can be absorbed through the skin.

Nihonium

Kōsuke Morita was part of the team of scientists that first made this element.

Nihonium is one of the most recent elements to be added to the periodic table. It was officially named in 2016. It is radioactive, has no known use, and only a few atoms have ever been made.

H																	He
Li	Be											B	C	N	O	F	Ne
Na	Mg											Al	Si	P	S	Cl	Ar
K	Ca	Sc	Ti	V	Cr	Mn	Fe	Co	Ni	Cu	Zn	Ga	Ge	As	Se	Br	Kr
Rb	Sr	Y	Zr	Nb	Mo	Tc	Ru	Rh	Pd	Ag	Cd	In	Sn	Sb	Te	I	Xe
Cs	Ba	La	Hf	Ta	W	Re	Os	Ir	Pt	Au	Hg	Tl	Pb	Bi	Po	At	Rn
Fr	Ra	Ac	Rf	Db	Sg	Bh	Hs	Mt	Ds	Rg	Cn	Nh	Fl	Mc	Lv	Ts	Og

Ce	Pr	Nd	Pm	Sm	Eu	Gd	Tb	Dy	Ho	Er	Tm	Yb	Lu
Th	Pa	U	Np	Pu	Am	Cm	Bk	Cf	Es	Fm	Md	No	Lr

Carbon group

The carbon group is a jumble! There is a familiar nonmetal (C) at the top, two metalloids (Si and Ge), and two metals (Sn and Pb) in the middle, and finally a very new, radioactive element (Fl) at the bottom.

Tin and lead are sometimes called "poor metals" because they have lower melting points and are softer and weaker than many other metals.

Allotropes

Carbon, silicon, and germanium are examples of elements that can take on more than one form. Such elements are called allotropes. For example, carbon can exist as diamond, graphite, and buckminsterfullerene.

Carbon

Carbon is arguably the most important of all the elements. All living things contain it, and carbon atoms are found in millions of naturally occurring compounds. Diamond and graphite are two common forms of carbon.

> » **Atomic number:** 6
> » **Category:** Carbon group
> » **Melting point:** 6,917 °F (3,825 °C)
> » **Discovery:** Prehistoric
> » **State at room temperature:** Solid

This sample of "glassy carbon" is dark and shiny.

Diamonds

Diamonds are just one form, or allotrope, of carbon. Diamond is the hardest known natural substance and is made up entirely of carbon atoms.

Glassy carbon is hard, has a low density, and is heat resistant.

The "lead" in pencils is actually graphite, another allotrope of carbon. The marks a pencil makes on paper are streaks of soft graphite.

Carbon is essential to all life. We call living material organic, so organic chemistry deals with carbon and its many compounds.

Silicon

Silicon is the second-most abundant element in the Earth's crust, behind only oxygen. The element is a semiconductor, which makes it a crucial part of the microchip and electronics industry.

A sample of pure silicon produced in a laboratory.

It does not look like this in nature; silicon is found in many minerals.

Germanium

The pure form of the element is shiny and brittle.

Like silicon, germanium is also an important semiconductor used in electronics. It is used in the production of high-quality lenses for cameras and microscopes. It is named after Germany, where it was discovered.

Ge   Fact file

» **Atomic number:** 32
» **Category:** Carbon group
» **Melting point:** 938 °C (1,721 °F)
» **Discovery:** 1886
» **State at room temperature:** Solid

Tin

Tin is a prehistoric element that has been known and used for many centuries. It is an important metal in alloys, especially bronze, which is a mixture of tin and copper.

Cassiterite, a mineral made mostly of tin and oxygen, is the most important source of tin.

Sn — Fact file

» **Atomic number:** 50
» **Category:** Carbon group
» **Melting point:** 232 °C (449 °F)
» **Discovery:** Prehistoric
» **State at room temperature:** Solid

Pb — Fact file

» **Atomic number:** 82
» **Category:** Carbon group
» **Melting point:** 327 °C (621 °F)
» **Discovery:** Prehistoric
» **State at room temperature:** Solid

Lead

Lead had an important role to play for centuries. It is dense, soft, and shaped easily. These are very useful properties; however, it was discovered that lead is toxic.

Lead is a dull, gray-colored metal that is resistant to corrosion.

Flerovium

Flerovium is one of the newest elements on the periodic table. It is a fiercely radioactive element, and only a few atoms have ever been created. Currently, it has no known uses outside of chemical research.

Element 114 is named after Georgy Flerov, a famous Russian scientist.

Fl — Fact file

» **Atomic number:** 114
» **Category:** Carbon group
» **Melting point:** Unknown
» **Discovery:** 1999
» **State at room temperature:** Solid

H																	He
Li	Be											B	C	**N**	O	F	Ne
Na	Mg											Al	Si	**P**	S	Cl	Ar
K	Ca	Sc	Ti	V	Cr	Mn	Fe	Co	Ni	Cu	Zn	Ga	Ge	**As**	Se	Br	Kr
Rb	Sr	Y	Zr	Nb	Mo	Tc	Ru	Rh	Pd	Ag	Cd	In	Sn	**Sb**	Te	I	Xe
Cs	Ba	La	Hf	Ta	W	Re	Os	Ir	Pt	Au	Hg	Tl	Pb	**Bi**	Po	At	Rn
Fr	Ra	Ac	Rf	Db	Sg	Bh	Hs	Mt	Ds	Rg	Cn	Nh	Fl	**Mc**	Lv	Ts	Og

Ce	Pr	Nd	Pm	Sm	Eu	Gd	Tb	Dy	Ho	Er	Tm	Yb	Lu
Th	Pa	U	Np	Pu	Am	Cm	Bk	Cf	Es	Fm	Md	No	Lr

Nitrogen group

The group 15 elements are sometimes called the *pnictogens*. That odd-sounding name comes from the Greek word *pnikta*, meaning "to choke" or "to suffocate." This is because you need oxygen, not nitrogen, to breathe.

A mixed bag

Group 15 contains metals, nonmetals, and semimetals. Apart from unreactive nitrogen—which is a gas at room temperature—the elements are solids. Phosphorus is a fiercely reactive element that burns brightly in the air.

Some elements in the nitrogen group are toxic, including phosphorus, arsenic, and antimony.

Nitrogen

Nitrogen is one of the diatomic elements, meaning that it goes around in pairs of atoms as a molecule of N_2. Under normal circumstances, it is an unreactive gas with an extremely strong bond between the two N atoms.

- » *Atomic number:* 7
- » *Category:* Nitrogen group
- » *Melting point:* $-346\,°F$ $(-210\,°C)$
- » *Discovery:* 1772
- » *State at room temperature:* Gas

Atmosphere

Nitrogen is an incredibly abundant gas on Earth. It makes up around 78 percent of the atmosphere, with oxygen around 21 percent, and other gases making up the remainder.

Liquid nitrogen is used to make ice cream.

Nitrogen is a gas at room temperature, so it is stored in glass.

Nitrogen is an essential element for plants. It is one of the main ingredients in fertilizers.

It is a colorless gas, but glows purple when electricity is passed through it.

This violet phosphorus can be made in the laboratory by heating red phosphorus.

Phosphorus

Phosphorus is an element that has several different forms called allotropes, distinguished by their different colors. White phosphorus is highly flammable and has been used in wartime to make smokescreens and bombs.

P — Fact file

» **Atomic number:** 15
» **Category:** Nitrogen group
» **Melting point:** 44 °C (111 °F)
» **Discovery:** 1669
» **State at room temperature:** Solid

Arsenic

Arsenic has a reputation as a poisonous element. It is very toxic to humans and has been used in rat poisons. Like phosphorus it comes in various colors, such as yellow, gray, and black.

This pure black arsenic crystal has been refined in a laboratory.

In its pure form, black arsenic is very shiny.

As — Fact file

» **Atomic number:** 33
» **Category:** Nitrogen group
» **Sublimes at:** 616 °C (1,141 °F)
» **Discovery:** c. 1250
» **State at room temperature:** Solid

Antimony

Antimony is a metalloid. Like phosphorus and arsenic, it has several different allotropes or forms. When it acts like a metal it looks and behaves like lead, and has long been mistaken for that metal.

Antimony is a silvery, hard element.

Sb Fact file

» **Atomic number:** 51
» **Category:** Nitrogen group
» **Melting point:** 631 °C (1,167 °F)
» **Discovery:** c. 1600 BCE
» **State at room temperature:** Solid

Bismuth often arranges in a distinct shape that looks like a staircase.

Bi Fact file

» **Atomic number:** 83
» **Category:** Nitrogen group
» **Melting point:** 271 °C (521 °F)
» **Discovery:** c. 1500
» **State at room temperature:** Solid

Bismuth

Bismuth is a metal with a low melting point that is used in alloys where that property is useful. It is used to plug fire sprinklers, where in a fire the plug will melt, releasing water.

Mc Fact file

» **Atomic number:** 115
» **Category:** Nitrogen group
» **Melting point:** Unknown
» **Discovery:** 2010
» **State at room temperature:** Solid

Moscovium

It is named after the city of Moscow, Russia.

Moscovium is a radioactive metal of which only a few atoms have ever been made. Because the atoms decay so quickly, very little is known about the chemistry of moscovium.

These six elements get more metallic as you go down the group.

| | | | | | | | | | | | | | | | | | H | | | | | | | | | | | | | | | | | | He |

H																	He
Li	Be											B	C	N	O	F	Ne
Na	Mg											Al	Si	P	S	Cl	Ar
K	Ca	Sc	Ti	V	Cr	Mn	Fe	Co	Ni	Cu	Zn	Ga	Ge	As	Se	Br	Kr
Rb	Sr	Y	Zr	Nb	Mo	Tc	Ru	Rh	Pd	Ag	Cd	In	Sn	Sb	Te	I	Xe
Cs	Ba	La	Hf	Ta	W	Re	Os	Ir	Pt	Au	Hg	Tl	Pb	Bi	Po	At	Rn
Fr	Ra	Ac	Rf	Db	Sg	Bh	Hs	Mt	Ds	Rg	Cn	Nh	Fl	Mc	Lv	Ts	Og

| Ce | Pr | Nd | Pm | Sm | Eu | Gd | Tb | Dy | Ho | Er | Tm | Yb | Lu |
| Th | Pa | U | Np | Pu | Am | Cm | Bk | Cf | Es | Fm | Md | No | Lr |

Oxygen group

Group 16 has an element at the top that is very familiar to us (oxygen) and one at the bottom that is one of the newest that we know very little about (livermorium). Collectively, they are called the chalcogens.

The group is a mixed bag that includes nonmetals (O and S), semimetals (Se and Te), and radioactive metals (Po and Lv).

Sand dunes in the Sahara Desert

Found in ores

The group 16 elements are quite reactive, especially oxygen and sulfur, which are found in many minerals and ores on Earth, including sand. Oxygen is the most abundant element on Earth, but only a few atoms of livermorium have ever been made.

76

Oxygen

This is one of the most abundant elements in Earth's crust. Oxygen and its compounds make up half of all the rocks and minerals on our planet. About 21 percent of the air we breathe is oxygen.

» **Atomic number:** 8
» **Category:** Oxygen group
» **Melting point:** −362 °F (−219 °C)
» **Discovery:** 1774
» **State at room temperature:** Gas

Auroras

Naturally occurring colorful displays of light that can be seen near the poles are called auroras. They are formed when particles from the sun enter Earth's atmosphere at high speed and hit oxygen and nitrogen atoms in the air.

Aurora Borealis

Liquid oxygen is mixed with liquid hydrogen to make rocket fuel.

This glass sphere holds pure oxygen.

- - When electricity is passed through oxygen, it emits a silver–blue glow.

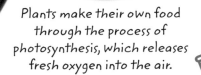

Plants make their own food through the process of photosynthesis, which releases fresh oxygen into the air.

Sulfur

Smelly and one of the most instantly recognizable elements, sulfur is widely used in medicines, fertilizers, and detergents. In ancient times, it was popularly known as "burning stone," because it burns quite easily.

» **Atomic number:** 16
» **Category:** Oxygen group
» **Melting point:** 239 °F (115 °C)
» **Discovery:** Prehistoric
» **State at room temperature:** Solid

Sulfur can often be found in volcanic mud and rock.

Pure sulfur has bright yellow crystals.

When onions are sliced, a sulfur compound is released into the air that can make your eyes water.

Its crystals can be up to 1.5 in (4 cm) long.

When melted, the yellow crystals turn blood red.

Sulfur springs

Sulfur occurs naturally in rocks and around hot springs. Leirhnjúkur, a volcano in Iceland, is known for its sulfur springs. The volcanic heat at this site has led to the formation of hot springs, mud pots, and fumaroles (vents), which are extremely hot!

Leirhnjúkur sulfur spring, Iceland

Selenium

Selenium is an essential element for human health, but in large amounts it can be poisonous, too. It is a semimetal, meaning that sometimes it acts like a typical metal and sometimes like a nonmetal.

Se Fact file

» **Atomic number:** 34
» **Category:** Oxygen group
» **Melting point:** 429 °F (221 °C)
» **Discovery:** 1817
» **State at room temperature:** Solid

Stained glass

Selenium has been used to make red pigments and glazes. It can also make glass orange and colorless. Such colored glasses are often seen in the windows of religious buildings.

The element is named after Selene, the Greek goddess of the moon.

Selenium can be consumed by eating several different foods. Brazil nuts are a good source.

The red form turns into the black form when heated at high temperatures.

Selenium comes in two different colors, silvery-gray and red.

Tellurium

Tellurium is a rare element. It is sometimes found on Earth in combination with gold, which itself is unusual, since gold forms few compounds. Tellurium in humans can be responsible for bad body odors!

» **Atomic number:** 52
» **Category:** Oxygen group
» **Melting point:** 841 °F (450 °C)
» **Discovery:** 1783
» **State at room temperature:** Solid

Tellurium is brittle, and silvery-white when in its crystal form.

As a semimetal, it has properties between that of a metal and a nonmetal.

Tellurium is named after *tellus*, the Latin name for "Earth."

Problem metal

Franz-Joseph Müller von Reichenstein discovered this element while he was mining in Transylvania, Romania. It was very hard to identify, and because of that he named it *aurum paradoxum* (paradoxical gold) or *metallum problematum* (problem metal).

In the body, tellurium is converted to a compound called dimethyl telluride, which smells like garlic and gives you "tellurium breath!"

Polonium

Polonium was discovered by Marie and Pierre Curie in France, but was named after Marie's homeland of Poland. It is a dangerous radioactive element and has been used as a poison in the past.

Uraninite is an ore used to source uranium, but it decays to give polonium too.

These ores contain very small amounts of polonium.

Po | Fact file

- » **Atomic number:** 84
- » **Category:** Oxygen group
- » **Melting point:** 489 °F (254 °C)
- » **Discovery:** 1898
- » **State at room temperature:** Solid

Livermorium

Livermorium wasn't officially named until 2012. The name comes from the Lawrence Livermore National Laboratory in California, US, where several new elements have been made.

Lv | Fact file

- » **Atomic number:** 116
- » **Category:** Oxygen group
- » **Melting point:** Unknown
- » **Discovery:** 2000
- » **State at room temperature:** Solid

Livermorium was first produced at the Joint Institute of Nuclear Research in Dubna, Russia, in 2000.

H																	He
Li	Be											B	C	N	O	F	Ne
Na	Mg											Al	Si	P	S	Cl	Ar
K	Ca	Sc	Ti	V	Cr	Mn	Fe	Co	Ni	Cu	Zn	Ga	Ge	As	Se	Br	Kr
Rb	Sr	Y	Zr	Nb	Mo	Tc	Ru	Rh	Pd	Ag	Cd	In	Sn	Sb	Te	I	Xe
Cs	Ba	La	Hf	Ta	W	Re	Os	Ir	Pt	Au	Hg	Tl	Pb	Bi	Po	At	Rn
Fr	Ra	Ac	Rf	Db	Sg	Bh	Hs	Mt	Ds	Rg	Cn	Nh	Fl	Mc	Lv	Ts	Og

			Ce	Pr	Nd	Pm	Sm	Eu	Gd	Tb	Dy	Ho	Er	Tm	Yb	Lu
			Th	Pa	U	Np	Pu	Am	Cm	Bk	Cf	Es	Fm	Md	No	Lr

Halogens

Group 17 contains some fascinating, dangerous, and colorful characters. You will find gases, solids, and a liquid, alongside a couple of extremely rare radioactive elements. Always looking to react, these elements are a wild bunch!

Chlorine, bromine, and iodine are all plentiful in nature, being found in the oceans and seaweed.

The salt-formers

The word *halogen* means "salt-forming" because the elements of group 17 readily react with metals to form compounds called salts, such as common table salt, sodium chloride.

Fluorine

Fluorine is a dangerous element! A poisonous and pale-yellow gas, it was responsible for killing several of the early chemists. Fluorine is the most reactive of all elements, forming many compounds in the process.

» **Atomic number:** 9
» **Category:** Halogen
» **Melting point:** −363 °F (−220 °C)
» **Discovery:** 1886
» **State at room temperature:** Gas

PTFE

NASA originally developed spacesuits coated in a fluorine-containing material because it was durable, strong, lightweight, flexible, and heat resistant. The material is called PTFE, better known as Teflon.

Normally pale yellow, fluorine appears purple in this electrical discharge tube.

Fluorine gas is not purple, but it gives off purple light when electricity is passed through it.

Fluorine has been used in water supplies and toothpaste to help protect teeth from decay.

Fluorine is sealed in glass because it is so dangerous and reactive.

Don't mix up fluorine's symbol (F), with flerovium's (Fl)!

Chlorine

Chlorine is used in the production of many chemicals, including plastics such as PVC. You may know it best as a disinfectant in drinking water and swimming pools, where it kills bacteria and viruses.

Pure yellow–green chlorine is enclosed in this glass sphere.

Cl   Fact file

» **Atomic number:** 17
» **Category:** Halogen
» **Melting point:** $-102\,^{\circ}C$ ($-151\,^{\circ}F$)
» **Discovery:** 1774
» **State at room temperature:** Gas

This glass sphere contains orange bromine vapor.

Bromine

Bromine is one of only two elements that is a liquid at room temperature (the other is mercury). It is one of the seven diatomic elements, meaning that its atoms travel in pairs as Br_2.

Br   Fact file

» **Atomic number:** 35
» **Category:** Halogen
» **Melting point:** $-7\,^{\circ}C$ ($19\,^{\circ}F$)
» **Discovery:** 1826
» **State at room temperature:** Liquid

Iodine

Iodine is found in seaweed. It is a key element for human health. Iodine sublimes at room temperature, meaning that it turns from a solid to a gas with no liquid phase.

Purple—black crystals of pure iodine can be seen inside this glass sphere.

Astatine was discovered by Emilio Segrè in 1940.

Astatine

Astatine is one of the rarest elements known. It is radioactive and decays so quickly that it is estimated that there are only a few grams of astatine on the entire planet!

Tennessine

Tennessine is one of the newest elements on the periodic table, only being discovered in 2010 and being named in 2016. It is radioactive, and only a few atoms have ever been made.

The element was discovered at Oak Ridge National Laboratory, Tennessee, US.

H																	He
Li	Be											B	C	N	O	F	Ne
Na	Mg											Al	Si	P	S	Cl	Ar
K	Ca	Sc	Ti	V	Cr	Mn	Fe	Co	Ni	Cu	Zn	Ga	Ge	As	Se	Br	Kr
Rb	Sr	Y	Zr	Nb	Mo	Tc	Ru	Rh	Pd	Ag	Cd	In	Sn	Sb	Te	I	Xe
Cs	Ba	La	Hf	Ta	W	Re	Os	Ir	Pt	Au	Hg	Tl	Pb	Bi	Po	At	Rn
Fr	Ra	Ac	Rf	Db	Sg	Bh	Hs	Mt	Ds	Rg	Cn	Nh	Fl	Mc	Lv	Ts	Og

| | | Ce | Pr | Nd | Pm | Sm | Eu | Gd | Tb | Dy | Ho | Er | Tm | Yb | Lu |
| | | Th | Pa | U | Np | Pu | Am | Cm | Bk | Cf | Es | Fm | Md | No | Lr |

You'll find the noble gases in group 18, on the far right of the periodic table.

Even though they are unreactive, a few compounds are known, mainly of krypton and xenon.

Noble gases

The first six elements in group 18 are colorless, odorless, tasteless, and unreactive gases. They are called the noble gases because they do not react with others, remaining distant! So far, we know very little about the most recently discovered noble gas, oganesson.

William Ramsey

The noble gases were some of the later elements to be discovered. William Ramsey was a key figure in their discovery. He won the 1904 Nobel Prize in Chemistry for his work with them.

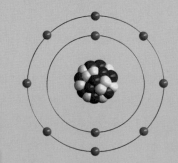

Noble gases have electronic configurations that make them rather unreactive.

Helium

Helium is the second lightest element—only hydrogen is lighter. It is a colorless, odorless, and tasteless gas. Helium is the second-most abundant element in the universe, but very little of it is found on Earth.

Helium is a colorless gas, but glows purple when electricity passes through it.

He | Fact file

- » **Atomic number:** 2
- » **Category:** Noble gas
- » **Melting point:** Unknown
- » **Discovery:** 1895
- » **State at room temperature:** Gas

Neon

Neon is a colorless gas, but glows bright red–orange when electricity is passed through it.

Neon is found throughout the universe, but it is extremely rare on Earth. Even so, the gas is very familiar to us because of its use in red–orange neon signs.

Ne | Fact file

- » **Atomic number:** 10
- » **Category:** Noble gas
- » **Melting point:** −415 °F (−248 °C)
- » **Discovery:** 1898
- » **State at room temperature:** Gas

Argon

The third-most abundant gas in the atmosphere, Argon is named after the Greek word *argos*, meaning "idle," because it is so unreactive. It is used in double-glazed windows, diving suits, and to protect exhibits at museums.

Argon gives off a shade of purple when electricity is passed through it.

Ar | Fact file

- » **Atomic number:** *18*
- » **Category:** *Noble gas*
- » **Melting point:** *−189 °C (−309 °F)*
- » **Discovery:** *1894*
- » **State at room temperature:** *Gas*

Krypton is colorless, but it glows blue–white when electricity is passed through it.

Krypton

This element got its name from the Greek word *kryptos*, meaning "hidden one." Krypton is rare and only present in tiny amounts in the air. It is used in lasers, digital cameras, and flashbulbs.

Kr | Fact file

- » **Atomic number:** *36*
- » **Category:** *Noble gas*
- » **Melting point:** *−157 °C (−251 °F)*
- » **Discovery:** *1898*
- » **State at room temperature:** *Gas*

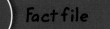

Xenon

Xe | Fact file

- » **Atomic number:** 54
- » **Category:** Noble gas
- » **Melting point:** −112 °C (−169 °F)
- » **Discovery:** 1898
- » **State at room temperature:** Gas

A rare gas, Xenon is colorless and odorless. It glows brightly when electricity is passed through it, so it is used in film projectors and car headlights.

Xenon glows blue when electricity runs through it.

Radon

Radon is found around volcanic springs.

Rn | Fact file

- » **Atomic number:** 86
- » **Category:** Noble gas
- » **Melting point:** −71 °C (−96 °F)
- » **Discovery:** 1900
- » **State at room temperature:** Gas

Radon is the only naturally occurring radioactive noble gas. A radioactive substance produces energy in the form of powerful and dangerous rays. So, breathing radon can be harmful.

Oganesson

Og | Fact file

- » **Atomic number:** 118
- » **Category:** Noble gas
- » **Melting point:** Unknown
- » **Discovery:** 2006
- » **State at room temperature:** Gas

This element was made by a team of Russian and American scientists. Named after Yuri Oganessian, a Russian physicist, this element has the largest atomic number and mass.

This Russian stamp shows Yuri Oganessian.

ARMENIA 2017 70

$^{249}Cf + ^{48}Ca$

| 118 Og 294 |
| 116 Lv 290 |
| 114 Fl 286 |
| 118 Og (294) oganessor |
| 112 Cn 282 |

ՅՈՒՐԻ ՀՈՎՀԱՆՆԻՍՅԱՆ YURI OGANESSIA

89

All together

This book shows off all the elements that have been discovered to date. Here you'll find a selection of the elements shown in the book.

Hydrogen
pg. 10–11

Lithium
pg. 13

Sodium
pg. 14

Potassium
pg. 15

Rubidium
pg. 16

Cesium
pg. 17

Francium
pg. 17

Beryllium
pg. 19

Magnesium
pg. 20

Calcium
pg. 21

Strontium
pg. 22

Barium
pg. 22

Radium
pg. 23

Scandium
pg. 25

Titanium
pg. 26

Vanadium
pg. 26

Chromium
pg. 27

Manganese
pg. 27

Iron
pg. 28

Cobalt
pg. 29

Nickel
pg. 30–31

Copper
pg. 32

Zinc
pg. 32

Yttrium
pg. 33

Zirconium
pg. 33

Niobium
pg. 33

Molybdenum
pg. 34

Technetium
pg. 34

Ruthenium
pg. 35

Rhodium
pg. 35

Palladium
pg. 35

Silver
pg. 36

Cadmium
pg. 37

Hafnium
pg. 37

Tantalum
pg. 37

Tungsten
pg. 38

Rhenium
pg. 38

Osmium
pg. 39

Iridium
pg. 39

Platinum
pg. 39

Gold
pg. 40–41

Mercury
pg. 42

Lanthanum
pg. 47

Cerium
pg. 47

Praseodymium
pg. 47

Neodymium
pg. 48

Promethium
pg. 48

Samarium
pg. 48

Europium
pg. 49

Gadolinium
pg. 49

Terbium
pg. 49

Dysprosium
pg. 50

Holmium
pg. 50

Erbium
pg. 50

Thulium
pg. 51

Ytterbium
pg. 51

Lutetium
pg. 51

Actinium
pg. 53

Thorium
pg. 54

Protactinium
pg. 54

Uranium
pg. 55

Neptunium
pg. 55

Plutonium
pg. 56–57

Americium
pg. 58

Californium
pg. 59

Boron
pg. 63

Aluminum
pg. 64

Gallium
pg. 65

Indium
pg. 66

Thallium
pg. 67

Carbon
pg. 69

Silicon
pg. 70

Germanium
pg. 70

Tin
pg. 71

Lead
pg. 71

Nitrogen
pg. 73

Phosphorus
pg. 74

Arsenic
pg. 74

Antimony
pg. 75

Bismuth
pg. 75

Oxygen
pg. 77

Sulfur
pg. 78

Selenium
pg. 79

Tellurium
pg. 80

Polonium
pg. 81

Fluorine
pg. 83

Chlorine
pg. 84

Bromine
pg. 84

Iodine
pg. 85

Helium
pg. 87

Neon
pg. 87

Argon
pg. 88

Krypton
pg. 88

Xenon
pg. 89

Radon
pg. 89

Glossary

abundant

existing or available in large amounts

acid

a substance with particular chemical properties, including dissolving some metals and neutralizing bases

alkali

see: base

allotrope

different forms of an element, for example, carbon existing as both diamond and graphite

alloy

a metal made by combining two or more elements, at least one of which is metallic

atmosphere

the collection of gases surrounding Earth or another planet

atom

the smallest part of an element that still has the same properties of the element

base

a substance with particular chemical properties, including neutralizing acids

brittle

hard but easy to break

catalyst

a substance that speeds up a chemical reaction

chemical reaction

a process in which one or more substances are converted into one or more different substances

compound

a substance in which two or more elements are combined in a fixed ratio

conductor

a material that allows an electrical current to flow through it easily

corrosion

the chemical deterioration of a material, often called rusting

decay

the process of an unstable nucleus emitting particles and transforming into a new nucleus

dense

a substance that has its material packed together tightly

diatomic

a particle that consists of two atoms

electron

a subatomic particle with a negative charge

elemental

occuring as an element

fertilizer

a chemical or natural substance added to soil or land to help plants grow

fission

a splitting of a large atomic nucleus into smaller nuclei

fusion

a combining of two small atomic nuclei to make a single, larger nucleus

galvanize

to add a protective layer to iron or steel in order to protect it from corrosion

gas

a type of matter that has no fixed shape, and can expand freely to fill a container

group

a column of the periodic table

infrared

a type of radiation just beyond the red end of the visible spectrum

irradiate

exposing someone or something to radiation, either for therapeutic purposes or to remove bacteria

isotope

atoms of a single element that differ only in the number of neutrons they possess

laboratory

a room or building used for scientific experiments, research, or teaching

liquid

a type of matter that is less rigid than a solid, so it can flow and does not have a specific shape

lubricant

a substance that helps to reduce friction between two surfaces

malleable

a material that is easily bent or pressed into a different shape without it breaking or cracking

melting point

the temperature at which a solid turns to a liquid

metalloid

elements whose properties are between those of a metal and a nonmetal

neutron

a subatomic particle with no charge

nucleus

the small, dense center of an atom, made up of protons and neutrons

ore

a naturally occuring material from which a metal or mineral can be extracted

particle

a very small piece of matter

period

a row on the periodic table

pigment

a substance that gives color to other materials

proton

a subatomic particle with a positive charge

radioactive

containing unstable atoms. The particles or rays these unstable atoms give off are types of radiation

state of matter

the three forms a substance can take: solid, liquid, and gas

semiconductor

a substance that has the conductivity between conductors and insulators. They are important components of electronic circuits

semimetal

see: metalloid

solid

a type of matter with a fixed volume and a fixed shape

subatomic

smaller than an atom

sublime

to change from a solid directly to a gas without passing through a liquid state

toxic

poisonous or harmful

ultraviolet

a type of radiation just beyond the violet end of the visible spectrum

visible spectrum

the part of the electromagnetic spectrum that can be detected by human eyes (red, orange, yellow, green, blue, indigo, and violet)

Index

Acknowledgments

Dorling Kindersley would like to thank the following people for their assistance in the preparation of this book: Amy Pimperton for proofreading and Susie Rae for the index, and Soumya Rampal for editorial assistance.

The publisher would like to thank the following for their kind permission to reproduce their photographs:

(Key: a-above; b-below/bottom; c-center; f-far; l-left; r-right; t-top)

1 Dreamstime.com: Kaipop (Border). 2–3 Dreamstime.com: Kaipop (Border). 2 Dorling Kindersley: RGB Research Limited (fbl). 3 Alamy Stock Photo: Ron Niebrugge (cb). Dorling Kindersley: Bob Gathany (br); RGB Research Limited (t, bc). Dreamstime.com: Raja Rc (tc). 4–5 Dreamstime.com: Kaipop (Border); Bjrn Wylezich. 5 Dreamstime.com: Daniela Spyropoulou / Dana (cr); (cra); Zoom-zoom (ca); Heathergreen (c); Aldona Griskeviciene (bc). 6–7 Dreamstime.com: Kaipop (Border). 6 Dreamstime.com: Andreykuzmin (cla); Martateron (tc); Valentina Razumova (cra). Science Photo Library: Giphotostock (crb). 7 Alamy Stock Photo: divgradcurl (clb). 8–9 Dreamstime.com: Kaipop (Border). 10–11 Dreamstime.com: Kaipop (Border). NASA: GSFC / SDO. 11 Dorling Kindersley: RGB Research Limited (cra). Dreamstime.com: Grafner (crb). 12 Dorling Kindersley: RGB Research Limited (cr). 13 Dorling Kindersley: RGB Research Limited (c). Dreamstime.com: Danil Roudenko / Danr13 (bc). 14 Alamy Stock Photo: GRANGER - Historical Picture Archive (br). Dorling Kindersley: RGB Research Limited (c). 15 Dorling Kindersley: RGB Research Limited (bl). Dreamstime.com: Valentyn75 (cr). 16 Dorling Kindersley: RGB Research Limited (c). Science Photo Library: (clb). 17 Dorling Kindersley: RGB Research Limited (t, br). 18 Dreamstime.com: Didesign021 (bl); Luchschen (cr). 19 Dorling Kindersley: Natural History Museum, London (cla); RGB Research Limited (b). NASA: Desiree Stover (cr). 20 Dorling Kindersley: RGB Research Limited (l). Dreamstime.com: Georgios Kollidas (br). 21 Dorling Kindersley: RGB Research Limited (r). Dreamstime.com: Vvoevale (cla). 22 Dorling Kindersley: RGB Research Limited (tr, br). 23 Alamy Stock Photo: IanDagnall Computing (br). 24 Getty Images / iStock: AlexeyKamenskiy (crb). 25 Alamy Stock Photo: Stefan Balaz (cra). Dreamstime.com: Dimitar Marinov (cr); Bjrn Wylezich (bl). 26 Dorling Kindersley: RGB Research Limited (ca, bl). 27 Dorling Kindersley: RGB Research Limited (tr). 28 Dorling Kindersley: RGB Research Limited (b). Dreamstime.com: Matthiashaas (cl). 29 Dorling Kindersley: RGB Research Limited (cra). Dreamstime.com: Pixs4u (br). 30–31 123RF.com. Dreamstime.com: Kaipop (Border). 31 Getty Images / iStock: kodachrome25 (cr). 32 Alamy Stock Photo: Susan E. Degginger (cra). Dorling Kindersley: RGB Research Limited (br). 33 Alamy Stock Photo: Phil Degginger (br). Dreamstime.com: Bjrn Wylezich (tr, cl). 34 Dorling Kindersley: RGB Research Limited (br). Dreamstime.com: Farbled (ca). 35 Alamy Stock Photo: Roberto Hunger (cr). Dorling Kindersley: RGB Research Limited (br). Dreamstime.com: Bjrn Wylezich (tc). 36 Alamy Stock Photo: Dinodia Photos RM (crb); David J. Green - technology (cr). Dorling Kindersley: Natural History Museum, London (b). 37 Alamy Stock Photo: Susan E. Degginger (ca). Dorling Kindersley: RGB Research Limited (cl). Shutterstock.com: RHJPhtotos (bc). 38 Dreamstime.com: Bjrn Wylezich (ca, bl). 39 Dorling Kindersley: RGB Research Limited (tr). Dreamstime.com: Roberto Junior (ca); Bjrn Wylezich (br). 40 Dreamstime.com: Jaroslav Moravcik (bl); Raja Rc (bc). 40–41 Dreamstime.com: Kaipop (Border); Bjrn Wylezich (c). 41 Alamy Stock Photo: Album (br). Dorling Kindersley: University of Pennsylvania Museum of Archaeology and Anthropology (cb). Dreamstime.com: Lateci (ca); Pablo631 (cra). 42 Dreamstime.com: Albund (ca). Science Photo Library: Universal History Archive / UIG (bl). 43 Alamy Stock Photo: Science History Images (ca, cr). Science Photo Library: (bc). 44 Alamy Stock Photo: ICP / incamerastock (br). Science Photo Library: David Parker (cla). 45 Dreamstime.com: Aurelko (bc); Nicku (cr). Science Photo Library: David Parker (ca). 46 Dreamstime.com: Aleksander Bedrin (ca). Science Photo Library: Dirk Wiersma (crb). 47 Dorling Kindersley: RGB Research Limited (tc, cr, bc). 48 Alamy Stock Photo: John Cancalosi (bc). Dorling Kindersley: RGB Research Limited (ca, cr). 49 Dorling Kindersley: RGB Research Limited (ca, bc). Dreamstime.

com: Luyag2 (cr). 50 Dorling Kindersley: RGB Research Limited (ca, cr, bc). 51 Dorling Kindersley: RGB Research Limited (ca, cr, bc). 52 NASA: JPL (cr). Science Photo Library: U.S. Dept. of Energy (bl). 53 Alamy Stock Photo: Burger / Phanie (cr). Dorling Kindersley: RGB Research Limited (b). 55 Dorling Kindersley: RGB Research Limited (tr, bl). 56–57 Dreamstime.com: Kaipop (Border). Science Photo Library: U.S. Dept. of Energy. 56 NASA: JPL-Caltech (bc). 57 Alamy Stock Photo: Maurice Savage (crb). Getty Images: Smith Collection / Gado (bl). 58 Alamy Stock Photo: Photo Researchers / Science History Images (bl). Dorling Kindersley: RGB Research Limited (cra). 59 Alamy Stock Photo: Aerial Archives (cra). Science Photo Library: U.S. Dept. of Energy (bl). 60 Alamy Stock Photo: Everett Collection Historical (bl); Ferdinand Schmutzer / Geopix / (ca). 61 Alamy Stock Photo: Pictorial Press Ltd (ca); RED / F1online digitale Bildagentur GmbH (cr). Getty Images: Smith Collection / Gado (bc). 62 Dreamstime.com: Andreadonetti (crb). NASA: (bl). 63 Dorling Kindersley: RGB Research Limited (crb). Getty Images / iStock: chengyuzheng (bl). 64 Dreamstime.com: Rideofthestorm (br); Bjrn Wylezich (c). 65 123RF.com: Maryna Pleshkun (cr). Dorling Kindersley: RGB Research Limited (cl). 66 Dorling Kindersley: RGB Research Limited (cla). Dreamstime.com: Prykhodov / iPad is a trademark of Apple Inc., registered in the U.S. and other countries (c); Bjrn Wylezich (b). 67 Dorling Kindersley: RGB Research Limited (cr). Getty Images: The Asahi Shimbun (br). 68 Dorling Kindersley: Science Museum, London (bc). 69 Dorling Kindersley: RGB Research Limited (b). Dreamstime.com: Ijp2726 (c); Kuruan (crb). 70 Dreamstime.com: Fireflyphoto (ca); Luyag2 (br). 71 Alamy Stock Photo: SPUTNIK (bc). Dorling Kindersley: RGB Research Limited (cr). 72 Science Photo Library: Charles D. Winters (bl). Shutterstock.com: VECTOR_X (crb). 73 123RF.com: unal ozmen (clb). Dorling Kindersley: RGB Research Limited (b). Getty Images: AleksandarGeorgiev (cl). 74 Dorling Kindersley: RGB Research Limited (cr). Science Photo Library: (cla). 75 Dorling Kindersley: RGB Research Limited (ca, cl). Dreamstime.com: Tomas1111 (br). 76 Dreamstime.com: Cristina Bernhardsen (bl); Nerthuz (crb). 77 Alamy Stock Photo: Ron Niebrugge (cl). Dorling Kindersley: RGB Research Limited (b). Dreamstime.com: Sandra Van Der Steen (crb). 78 Alamy Stock Photo: blickwinkel / McPHOTO / WLF (br). 79 Dreamstime.com: Draftmode (cra); Florin Seitan (cl); Bjrn Wylezich (c). 80 Alamy Stock Photo: History and Art Collection (bl). Dreamstime.com: Bjrn Wylezich (c). 81 Alamy Stock Photo: SPUTNIK (clb). Dreamstime.com: Jan Vlk (ca). 82 Alamy Stock Photo: David Cook / blueshiftstudios (cr). Dreamstime.com: Atman (b). 83 Dorling Kindersley: Bob Gathany (clb). Dreamstime.com: Kim Christensen (c). 84 Dorling Kindersley: RGB Research Limited (tr, bl). 85 Alamy Stock Photo: SuperStock (bc). Dorling Kindersley: RGB Research Limited (tc). Getty Images: Keystone (cl). 86 Alamy Stock Photo: Dimitar Todorov (crb). Getty Images: SSPL (bl). 87 Dorling Kindersley: RGB Research Limited (tr, bl). 88 Dorling Kindersley: RGB Research Limited (tr, bl). 89 Dorling Kindersley: RGB Research Limited (tr, cl). Dreamstime.com: Fmua (br). 90 Alamy Stock Photo: Susan E. Degginger (4:1, 5:5); Phil Degginger (4:5); Roberto Hunger (5:2). Dorling Kindersley: Natural History Museum, London (5:4); RGB Research Limited (1:1, 1:2, 1:3, 1:4, 1:5, 1:6, 1:7, 2:1, 2:2, 2:3, 2:4, 2:5, 3:1, 3:2, 3:3, 3:5, 3:6, 4:2, 4:7, 5:3, 5:6, 6:3). Dreamstime.com: Albund (6:7); Bjrn Wylezich (2:7); Bjrn Wylezich (4:3, 4:4, 5:1, 6:1, 6:2, 6:5, 6:6); Farbled (4:6); Roberto Junior (6:4). Getty Images / iStock: kodachrome25 (3:7). Shutterstock.com: RHJPhtotos (5:7). 90–91 Dreamstime.com: Kaipop (Border). 91 Alamy Stock Photo: John Cancalosi (1:6). Dorling Kindersley: RGB Research Limited (1:1, 1:2, 1:3, 1:4, 1:5, 1:7, 2:2, 2:3, 2:4, 2:5, 2:6, 2:7, 3:1, 3:2, 3:5, 3:6, 4:1, 4:3, 4:5, 4:7, 5:1, 5:5, 5:6, 6:1, 6:2, 6:3, 6:4, 7:3, 7:4, 7:5, 7:6, 7:7, 8:1, 8:2, 8:3, 8:4). Dreamstime.com: Kim Christensen (7:2); Luyag2 (2:1, 5:3); Bjrn Wylezich (4:4, 4:6, 6:6, 6:7); Fireflyphoto (5:2); Jan Vlk (7:1). Science Photo Library: (5:7); U.S. Dept. of Energy (3:7, 4:2). 92 Dreamstime.com: Albund (tr); Tomas1111 (bl).

92–93 Dreamstime.com: Kaipop (Border). 93 Dorling Kindersley: RGB Research Limited (fbr). Dreamstime.com: Sandra Van Der Steen (br). 94 Alamy Stock Photo: RED / F1online digitale Bildagentur GmbH (br). Dorling Kindersley: RGB Research Limited (tc). 94–95 Dreamstime.com: Kaipop (Border). 95 Dorling Kindersley: Natural History Museum, London (crb). Dreamstime.com: Pixs4u (cra). 96 Dreamstime.com: Kaipop (Border); Jaroslav Moravcik (br).

Cover images: Front: Alamy Stock Photo: Susan E. Degginger cr; Dorling Kindersley: Natural History Museum, London cla/ (Morganite), RGB Research Limited tc, tr, cla, ca, cra/ (Bromine), fcra, cl, cb, bl, bc; Dreamstime.com: Albund crb, Fireflyphoto cra, Valentina Razumova tl, Bjrn Wylezich ca/ (Gold nugget), cb/ (Aluminum); Science Photo Library: Dirk Wiersma clb; Shutterstock.com: RHJPhtotos cra/ (tantalum); Back: Alamy Stock Photo: Roberto Hunger clb; Dorling Kindersley: RGB Research Limited ftl, tc, tr/ (Vanadium), tr, fcla, cla/ (Chlorine), cl, c, cr, c/ (Terbium), cr/ (Palladium), fcr, cb, bl, cb/ (Barium), cb/ (Neon), bc; Dreamstime.com: Luyag2 br/ (Germanium), Jan Vlk tl, Bjrn Wylezich crb, Bjrn Wylezich cla, ca, ca/ (Tungsten); Spine: Dorling Kindersley: RGB Research Limited t, cb, cb/ (Francium), b; Dreamstime.com: Roberto Junior cb/ (Iridium), Bjrn Wylezich ca.

All other images © Dorling Kindersley

About the author

Adrian Dingle is a chemistry educator and author. An Englishman, he now lives in the United States. He is the creator of the award-winning chemistry website Adrian Dingle's Chemistry Pages at *www.adriandingleschemistrypages.com* and holds a BSc. (Hons.) Chemistry, and a Postgraduate Certificate in Education (Secondary Chemistry), both from the University of Exeter in England. He's a lifelong fan of Leeds United football club, and a former season ticket holder.